The DEM Manual

The DEM Manual

Frankie Mooney
5051 Worldwide (5051 Publishing)
Glasgow

Contents

Preface

In the vast landscape of human interaction, communication stands as the cornerstone of our connections, decisions, and shared understanding. For over twenty years, I have explored the depths of personal development, NLP, and hypnosis, guiding individuals toward greater self-awareness and mastery over their lives. These experiences taught me that communication is not just about exchanging words—it's about eliciting responses, shaping perceptions, and creating meaningful interactions. However, as I navigated these fields, I recognized a gap—a need for a model that could bridge intuitive practices with scientific rigor, a model that could be universally applied yet remain deeply personal.

This recognition led to the creation of the Dual-Mode Elicitation Model™, or DEM.

DEM is rooted in the idea that communication operates in two primary modes: Directive and Exploratory. These modes are not separate entities but rather two sides of the same coin, constantly interacting to shape our understanding of the world and our place within it. The Directive Mode focuses on guiding the conversation, offering clear instructions, and driving toward a specific outcome. The Exploratory Mode, on the other hand, encourages open-ended questioning, curiosity, and discovery. Together, these modes create a dynamic interplay that allows for more effective and responsive communication.

As I transitioned from the realms of NLP and hypnosis to a more scientifically grounded approach, DEM became not just a tool but a framework—a framework that integrates principles from cognitive psychology, AI, and therapeutic communication. It offers a way to harness the power of both structured guidance and open exploration in a way that is adaptable to various fields, from education and therapy to AI development and beyond.

In this manual, you will find an in-depth exploration of DEM, supported by research, practical applications, and case studies. But more than that, I hope you find a model that resonates with your own experiences and challenges you to think differently about communication. Whether you are a researcher looking to expand your methodologies, a practitioner seeking new tools, or simply someone interested in the art and science of communication, DEM offers a pathway to more intentional, integrative interactions.

As you read through the pages of this manual, I invite you to engage with DEM not just as a set of techniques, but as a lens through which to view the complexities of human communication. Consider how the Directive and Exploratory Modes operate in your own life, and how you might use them to foster deeper connections, more insightful inquiries, and ultimately, a greater understanding of those around you.

My journey to DEM has been one of discovery, reflection, and transformation. It has taken me from the intuitive practices of personal development to the structured realms of science, and it is my hope that DEM will serve as a bridge for you as well—a bridge between what we know and what we have yet to discover.

Thank you for joining me on this journey.

Best regards,

Frankie Mooney

Developer of the Dual-Mode Elicitation Model™

I.

Introduction: Setting the Stage for DEM

Overview of the Dual Mode Elicitation Model (DEM)

The Dual Mode Elicitation Model (DEM) represents a significant evolution in communication theory, merging insights from cognitive psychology, neuroscience, communication theory, artificial intelligence (AI), and other fields to create a comprehensive framework for optimizing human interaction across a variety of contexts. DEM is particularly relevant in today's world, where the demands for effective communication are rapidly increasing due to the complexities of modern technology, globalized communication, and the integration of AI into everyday life. This introduction aims to establish the foundational significance of the DEM Model, discussing its interdisciplinary roots, its application across various domains, and how it addresses contemporary communication challenges.

The Importance of Effective Communication in Modern Contexts

Effective communication is crucial in navigating the complexities of modern life, whether in guiding AI systems, enhancing educational methods, or improving therapeutic practices. Communication must be clear yet flexible, precise yet adaptable, to meet the diverse needs of different contexts (LeDoux, 2000). The DEM Model addresses these challenges by integrating directive and exploratory communication modes, allowing communicators to adapt their strategies dynamically based on situational demands.

Introducing the DEM Model

The DEM Model is a dynamic framework designed to optimize communication by integrating two primary modes: the Directive Mode and the Exploratory Mode.

- **Directive Mode**: Characterized by structured, goal-oriented communication, the Directive Mode is essential when clarity and precision are paramount. It aligns closely with Daniel Kahneman's concept of "System 1" thinking, which is fast, automatic, and intuitive (Kahneman, 2011). This mode is particularly effective in situations where specific outcomes need to be achieved, such as in procedural instructions, decision-making processes, and structured educational settings.

- **Exploratory Mode**: In contrast, the Exploratory Mode fosters open-ended communication, creativity, and adaptability. It corresponds to "System 2" thinking, which is slow, deliberate, and logical (Kahneman, 2011). This mode is crucial in contexts that require innovation, problem-solving, and the exploration of new ideas, such as in brainstorming sessions, therapeutic dialogues, and adaptive learning environments.

The DEM Model's unique contribution lies in its ability to dynamically integrate these two modes, allowing communicators to adapt their approach based on the specific needs of the context, audience, and desired outcomes.

Interdisciplinary Foundations of the DEM Model

The DEM Model is grounded in a rich interdisciplinary foundation, drawing on cutting-edge research from multiple fields to enhance its robustness and applicability.

1. **Cognitive Psychology**:

   - Kahneman's dual-process theory, particularly the distinction between System 1 and System 2 thinking, forms the backbone of the DEM Model (Kahneman, 2011). This theory explains how individuals process information and make decisions, providing a psychological basis for the Directive and Exploratory Modes. The DEM Model leverages these insights to optimize communication by aligning with the cognitive processes of the human brain.

- John Sweller's Cognitive Load Theory further informs the Directive Mode by emphasizing the need to manage cognitive resources effectively during structured tasks (Sweller, 1988). This is particularly relevant in educational settings, where reducing cognitive load can enhance learning outcomes.

2. **General Semantics**:

- Alfred Korzybski's *Science and Sanity* introduces the concept of General Semantics, which explores the relationship between language, thought, and behavior (Korzybski, 1933). General Semantics emphasizes how language shapes our perception of reality, a principle that is central to the Directive Mode of DEM. By structuring language effectively, the Directive Mode influences how information is communicated and understood, ensuring clarity and precision.

3. **Biological Underpinnings: Neuroscience and Evolutionary Psychology**:

- Neuroscience provides critical insights into the biological mechanisms that underlie the DEM Model. Eric Kandel's research on neural plasticity, for example, highlights the brain's capacity to adapt and reorganize itself, aligning with the flexibility inherent in the Exploratory Mode (Kandel, 2006).
- Joseph LeDoux's work on the neuroscience of emotion regulation is particularly relevant to DEM, as it explores how emotional responses can be managed to facilitate effective communication (LeDoux, 2000). This understanding is crucial for maintaining emotional control in high-stress situations, a key aspect of the Directive

Mode.

- Evolutionary psychology contributes to our understanding
  of how communication strategies have evolved to address
  different environmental challenges, informing both the
  Directive and Exploratory Modes. These insights help
  explain the adaptive nature of communication and its role
  in survival and social cohesion (Cosmides & Tooby, 1992).

4. **Embodied Cognition**:

- Shaun Gallagher's research on embodied cognition
  emphasizes the role of the body in shaping the mind,
  suggesting that cognitive processes are deeply influenced
  by our physical interactions with the world (Gallagher,
  2005). This perspective enriches the Exploratory Mode of
  DEM by highlighting the importance of considering
  physical context and sensory experiences in
  communication.

5. **Consciousness Studies**:

- William James, a pioneer in the study of consciousness,
  provides foundational insights into the nature of conscious
  experience and its influence on human behavior (James,
  1890). His work underscores the dynamic interplay
  between conscious and unconscious processes, a concept
  integral to the DEM Model's ability to facilitate both
  structured and exploratory communication.

Broad Applicability of the DEM Model

The versatility of the DEM Model is one of its most significant
strengths, making it applicable across a wide range of fields:

- **Artificial Intelligence (AI) Development**: DEM guides the
  development of AI systems that require both structured
  interactions and adaptability. For instance, in human-

computer interaction, AI systems can employ the Directive Mode to provide clear instructions while using the Exploratory Mode to engage in more nuanced, context-sensitive dialogues. This dual approach is particularly relevant in areas such as natural language processing, where AI must navigate the complexities of human language (Hinton et al., 2015).

- **Education**: DEM enhances teaching methods by allowing educators to balance structured instruction with open-ended exploration. This approach improves student engagement, fosters critical thinking, and adapts to diverse learning styles. For example, in a blended learning environment, the Directive Mode can be used to deliver core content, while the Exploratory Mode encourages students to explore and apply their knowledge in creative ways (Sweller, 1988).

- **Therapy**: DEM improves therapeutic communication by helping therapists balance directive guidance with exploratory inquiry, leading to more effective therapeutic outcomes. The model allows therapists to adapt their communication strategies based on the client's needs and progress, fostering a deeper therapeutic relationship and enhancing client outcomes (LeDoux, 2000).

- **Strategic Communication**: In fields such as marketing, public relations, and organizational communication, DEM can be applied to develop strategies that are both clear and adaptable. By leveraging both Directive and Exploratory Modes, communicators can craft messages that resonate with diverse audiences and adapt to changing circumstances. This is particularly important in crisis communication, where the ability to switch between modes can be crucial for managing public perception (Bernays, 1928).

Practical Application: Embedded Examples and Conceptual Framework

To illustrate the practical application of DEM, consider the following example in healthcare communication:

- **Healthcare Communication Example**: In a patient-centered care setting, a healthcare provider might use the Directive Mode to clearly explain a treatment plan, ensuring that the patient understands the necessary steps. Simultaneously, the provider can employ the Exploratory Mode to engage the patient in a discussion about their concerns and preferences, allowing for a more personalized approach to care. This dynamic integration ensures that communication is both effective and empathetic, leading to better patient outcomes and increased satisfaction (Gallagher, 2005).

The conceptual framework of DEM is designed to be dynamic, balancing the Directive and Exploratory Modes to create an adaptive communication strategy. This framework evolves based on the needs of the situation, the goals of the communication, and the responses of the participants, making it highly versatile across different contexts.

Future Research and Open Questions

As with any model, DEM offers opportunities for further research and development:

- **Integration of Unconscious Processes**: Future research could explore how unconscious processes and phenomenological control can be more deeply integrated into communication strategies. Understanding how these elements influence decision-making and interaction can lead to more effective applications of DEM, particularly in fields like AI, where the goal is to emulate human-like communication (Carhart-Harris et al., 2014).
- **Emerging Technologies**: As AI and communication technologies continue to evolve, new opportunities will arise to apply the DEM Model in ways that enhance human-computer interaction, improve educational tools, and advance therapeutic practices. Research into how DEM can be integrated with emerging technologies like virtual reality (VR),

augmented reality (AR), and neuromorphic computing will be crucial for its future development (Hinton et al., 2015).

Conclusion

The Dual Mode Elicitation Model (DEM) represents a significant advancement in communication theory, offering a robust and adaptable framework for optimizing interaction across diverse contexts. By integrating insights from cognitive psychology, neuroscience, communication theory, embodied cognition, and consciousness studies, DEM provides a comprehensive approach to communication that balances structure with flexibility. As the manual progresses, subsequent chapters will delve deeper into the theoretical foundations, practical applications, and future implications of DEM, offering a detailed guide for academics, professionals, and researchers looking to apply this model in their work.

2.

The Theoretical Foundations of DEM

Introduction

The Dual Mode Elicitation Model (DEM) is built upon a rich and diverse theoretical foundation that integrates insights from cognitive psychology, neuroscience, communication theory, and General Semantics. This chapter explores these foundational theories, illustrating how each contributes to the development and application of DEM. By examining these interdisciplinary connections, we can understand the robustness of DEM and its relevance across various fields, from artificial intelligence to therapeutic practices.

Cognitive Psychology: Dual-Process Theory and Cognitive Load

Cognitive psychology offers crucial insights into how individuals process information and make decisions, which directly informs the design of the DEM Model.

- **Dual-Process Theory (Kahneman, 2011):**
  - Daniel Kahneman's dual-process theory serves as the bedrock of DEM, distinguishing between two types of cognitive processes: System 1 and System 2. System 1 is fast, intuitive, and automatic, aligning with the Directive Mode of DEM, where structured and goal-oriented communication is required . System 2, on the other hand, is slow, deliberate, and logical, reflecting the Exploratory Mode of DEM, where open-ended communication and adaptability is emphasized.
  - This distinction is critical for understanding how DEM can be applied in various contexts, allowing for a balance between efficiency and flexibility in communication

strategies.

- **Cognitive Load Theory (Sweller, 1988):**
  - John Sweller's Cognitive Load Theory highlights the limitations of working memory and the importance of managing cognitive resources effectively. The Directive Mode of DEM is informed by this theory, as it aims to reduce extraneous cognitive load by structuring information clearly and concisely.
  - In educational settings, for example, applying the Directive Mode helps optimize learning by minimizing unnecessary cognitive demands, allowing students to focus on core content.

Neuroscience: Neural Plasticity, Emotion Regulation, and the Modular Brain

Neuroscience provides a biological basis for understanding the mechanisms underlying the DEM Model, particularly in how the brain processes and adapts to information.

- **Neural Plasticity (Kandel, 2006):**
  - Eric Kandel's research on neural plasticity underscores the brain's ability to reorganize itself in response to new experiences. This adaptability is central to the Exploratory Mode of DEM, where communication is fluid and responsive to changing contexts.
  - In practical applications, such as adaptive learning technologies, the Exploratory Mode allows systems to adjust based on user feedback, mirroring the brain's plasticity.
- **Emotion Regulation (LeDoux, 2000):**
  - Joseph LeDoux's work on the neuroscience of emotion regulation is integral to both modes of DEM. The Directive Mode benefits from an understanding of how emotions can be managed to maintain clarity and focus in

communication. Conversely, the Exploratory Mode leverages emotional dynamics to foster creativity and engagement.

  ◦ Emotion regulation is particularly relevant in high-stress environments, such as crisis management or therapeutic settings, where maintaining or harnessing emotional states can significantly impact communication outcomes.

- **The Modular Brain (Gazzaniga, 2000):**

  ◦ Michael Gazzaniga's research on the modularity of the brain suggests that different cognitive processes are compartmentalized yet can be integrated for complex tasks. This modular approach parallels how DEM integrates the Directive and Exploratory Modes, allowing for both structured and flexible communication as needed.

  ◦ For instance, in AI systems, the modularity concept is applied by integrating specialized algorithms that handle directive tasks while others manage exploratory interactions, thereby creating a more adaptive and responsive system.

Communication Theory and General Semantics

The role of language and communication in shaping reality is a central theme in DEM, particularly through the lens of General Semantics.

- **General Semantics (Korzybski, 1933):**

  ◦ Alfred Korzybski's *Science and Sanity* introduced General Semantics, a discipline that explores how language influences thought and behavior. This theory is foundational to the Directive Mode of DEM, where precise language is used to guide thought and action effectively.

  ◦ The principle that "the map is not the territory" reflects the idea that language (the map) is not the reality (the territory), but it shapes our perception of it. In DEM, this concept is applied to ensure that communication is not only clear but also accurately represents the intended reality.

- **Behaviorism and Social Learning Theory (Skinner, 1957; Bandura, 1977):**
  - B.F. Skinner's behaviorism and Albert Bandura's social learning theory provide additional insights into how communication strategies can influence behavior. The Directive Mode often employs behaviorist principles by using reinforcement to shape communication outcomes. Meanwhile, the Exploratory Mode benefits from social learning theory, which emphasizes learning through observation and interaction.
  - In educational technologies, these theories inform how DEM can be used to design systems that both instruct (Directive) and allow for exploration and learning through interaction (Exploratory).

Embodied Cognition and the Role of the Body in Communication

Embodied cognition, as researched by Shaun Gallagher, emphasizes the importance of physical experience in shaping cognitive processes, which is particularly relevant to the Exploratory Mode of DEM.

- **Embodied Cognition (Gallagher, 2005):**
  - Gallagher's work highlights how our cognitive processes are deeply intertwined with our physical bodies and interactions with the environment. This perspective is crucial for understanding the Exploratory Mode of DEM, where communication is often influenced by physical context and non-verbal cues.
  - For example, in face-to-face interactions or virtual reality environments, the Exploratory Mode of DEM can be employed to create more immersive and contextually aware communication experiences.

Consciousness Studies: Contributions of William James

The contributions of William James to the understanding of consciousness provide a philosophical and psychological foundation for DEM.

- **William James and Consciousness (James, 1890):**
  - William James' exploration of consciousness offers insights into how conscious and unconscious processes influence communication. His idea of the "stream of consciousness" aligns with the fluidity of the Exploratory Mode in DEM, where communication flows and adapts to the ongoing context.
  - James' work also supports the integration of Directive and Exploratory Modes by acknowledging that both structured (directive) and unstructured (exploratory) thought processes are essential for navigating complex communication scenarios.

Interdisciplinary Integration: The Convergence of Theories in DEM

The DEM Model's strength lies in its interdisciplinary nature, synthesizing insights from cognitive psychology, neuroscience, communication theory, and other fields to create a versatile framework for communication.

- **Interdisciplinary Synthesis:**
  - DEM is not just a theoretical model but a sophisticated cognitive framework that benefits from the convergence of multiple disciplines. For example, the integration of Kahneman's dual-process theory with Kandel's research on neural plasticity illustrates how cognitive processes and brain adaptability work together in communication.
  - Similarly, the combination of General Semantics with embodied cognition shows how language and physical experience jointly shape communication outcomes,

reinforcing the versatility of the DEM Model.

- **Future Implications**:

  - As fields such as AI, neuroscience, and communication
    continue to evolve, DEM's interdisciplinary foundation
    positions it as a critical framework for future research and
    application. Understanding how these disciplines interact
    and inform one another will be essential for advancing
    both theoretical knowledge and practical applications of
    DEM.
  - Additionally, the ethical implications of integrating DEM
    into AI systems, particularly concerning autonomy and
    bias, will require ongoing exploration and discourse.

Conclusion

Chapter 1 has provided a comprehensive overview of the theoretical foundations of the Dual Mode Elicitation Model (DEM). By integrating insights from cognitive psychology, neuroscience, communication theory, General Semantics, and consciousness studies, DEM emerges as a robust and adaptable framework for optimizing communication. The interdisciplinary nature of DEM not only enhances its theoretical underpinnings but also ensures its applicability across a wide range of domains, from AI development to therapeutic practices. As we move forward, the subsequent chapters will delve deeper into the practical applications and future implications of DEM, offering a detailed guide for researchers, professionals, and academics.

3.

The Directive Mode

Introduction

The Directive Mode within the Dual Mode Elicitation Model (DEM) emphasizes structured, goal-oriented communication, which is essential in contexts where clarity, precision, and efficiency are paramount. This chapter delves into the theoretical foundations of the Directive Mode, exploring how it aligns with key psychological, linguistic, and behavioral principles. We will examine its application across various fields, from education to artificial intelligence (AI), and discuss the future directions for research in this area. The Directive Mode's relevance is underscored by its ability to guide decision-making, enhance learning, and improve the effectiveness of communication in both human and machine interactions.

Theoretical Foundations of the Directive Mode

The Directive Mode is grounded in several foundational theories that explain how structured communication can optimize cognitive processes and influence behavior.

- **System 1 Processing (Kahneman, 2011):**
  - Daniel Kahneman's concept of System 1 processing, introduced in Thinking, Fast and Slow, is central to the Directive Mode. System 1 is characterized by fast, automatic, and intuitive thinking, which aligns with the structured, goal-oriented nature of the Directive Mode. This mode is critical in scenarios where rapid response, confidence, and decisiveness are necessary, such as in crisis management, sales, leadership, and behavioral influence.The Directive Mode leverages System 1 processing to:

Deliver clear, confident, and immediate communication. Reduce cognitive load on the listener, making suggestions easier to accept.

Optimize suggestion-based interactions where rapid compliance or decisiveness is needed.

- **Cognitive Load Theory (Sweller, 1988):**

  - John Sweller's Cognitive Load Theory (CLT) provides a framework for understanding how structured communication can reduce cognitive overload, particularly in educational contexts. CLT suggests that the human brain has a limited capacity for processing information, and effective instructional design should aim to minimize unnecessary cognitive load.

  - In the Directive Mode, communication is structured to present information in a way that is easy to process, helping learners focus on the essential content without being overwhelmed. This approach enhances learning outcomes by ensuring that cognitive resources are allocated efficiently.

- **Behaviorism and Reinforcement (Skinner, 1957):**

  - B.F. Skinner's behaviorism emphasizes the role of reinforcement in shaping behavior. The Directive Mode often employs behaviorist principles by using reinforcement to guide communication outcomes. For example, in educational settings, structured feedback is used to reinforce correct responses, helping learners internalize the desired behavior.

  - This approach is also applicable in AI systems, where reinforcement learning algorithms can be designed to optimize decision-making by reinforcing successful strategies.

Structured Communication in Practice: Language, Thought, and Action

The Directive Mode's emphasis on structured communication is further supported by linguistic theories that explore the relationship between language, thought, and behavior.

- **Language in Thought and Action (Hayakawa, 1949)**:
    - S.I. Hayakawa's *Language in Thought and Action* highlights the importance of language as a tool for structuring thought and guiding action. According to Hayakawa, precise language use is critical for effective communication, particularly in contexts where misunderstanding could have significant consequences.
    - The Directive Mode aligns with Hayakawa's emphasis on clarity and precision in language. In practical applications, this might involve using standardized terminology in legal documents or employing clear instructional language in educational materials.
- **Explainable AI Frameworks**:
    - In the context of AI, the Directive Mode plays a crucial role in the development of explainable AI (XAI). XAI frameworks are designed to ensure that AI systems provide clear, understandable explanations for their decisions, making them more transparent and trustworthy to users (Gunning et al., 2019).
    - The Directive Mode supports XAI by structuring AI outputs in a way that is easily interpretable by humans. This is particularly important in fields like healthcare or finance, where the consequences of AI decisions can be significant.

Practical Applications of the Directive Mode

The Directive Mode is applied across a wide range of fields, each benefiting from its structured, goal-oriented approach to communication.

- **Education**:

- In educational settings, the Directive Mode is essential for delivering structured, curriculum-based instruction. It is particularly effective in teaching foundational skills, where clear and precise guidance is necessary for student understanding. For instance, in mathematics education, the Directive Mode ensures that students receive unambiguous instructions on problem-solving methods, which are reinforced through practice and feedback (Sweller, 1988).
  - Additionally, the Directive Mode is integral to instructional design, where lessons are structured to manage cognitive load effectively, enhancing the retention and application of knowledge.

- **Artificial Intelligence**:

  - The Directive Mode is pivotal in AI systems that require precision and reliability. For example, in automated customer service bots, the Directive Mode ensures that the AI provides clear and concise responses to user queries, reducing the likelihood of miscommunication. In Explainable AI (XAI), the Directive Mode helps AI systems articulate their decision-making processes in a way that is understandable to users, thereby building trust and facilitating human-AI collaboration (Gunning et al., 2019).
  - Another application is in AI-driven diagnostics in healthcare, where the Directive Mode ensures that medical advice is communicated with the necessary clarity and accuracy to avoid potentially life-threatening misunderstandings.

- **Behavioral Economics and Nudge Theory (Thaler & Sunstein, 2008)**:

  - The Directive Mode is also relevant in the field of behavioral economics, particularly in the context of nudge theory. Nudge theory, as developed by Richard Thaler and Cass Sunstein, involves subtly guiding individuals towards certain behaviors without restricting their freedom of choice. The Directive Mode aligns with this approach by structuring communication in a way that nudges individuals towards desired outcomes.

- ○ For example, in public health campaigns, the Directive Mode might be used to design messages that encourage healthier lifestyle choices by clearly outlining the benefits of specific behaviors, such as vaccination or regular exercise.

Evolutionary Psychology and Directive Communication

Evolutionary psychology provides insights into why structured, goal-oriented communication is effective in certain contexts, particularly those involving survival and social cohesion.

- **Evolutionary Perspectives on Communication:**
  - ○ From an evolutionary standpoint, the ability to communicate directives effectively has likely played a critical role in human survival. Clear, goal-oriented communication would have been essential in coordinating group activities, such as hunting or defense, where ambiguity could lead to failure or danger (Cosmides & Tooby, 1992).
  - ○ In modern contexts, the Directive Mode continues to be important in situations where clear communication is essential for achieving specific goals, such as in military operations, emergency response, or leadership within organizations.
- **Application in Leadership and Organizational Communication:**
  - ○ In leadership, the Directive Mode is often used to establish clear expectations and directives that align with organizational goals. Leaders who communicate effectively using the Directive Mode can enhance team performance by providing clear guidance, setting expectations, and

ensuring that everyone is aligned with the organization's objectives (Bass, 1990).
  - Similarly, in crisis communication, the Directive Mode is critical for conveying important information quickly and clearly, helping to manage public perception and maintain order.

Challenges and Limitations of the Directive Mode

While the Directive Mode offers significant benefits, it also presents certain challenges and limitations that must be managed to ensure effective communication.

- **Over-Structuring Communication**:
  - One of the primary risks of the Directive Mode is the potential for over-structuring communication, which can lead to rigidity and a lack of responsiveness. In dynamic environments where adaptability is crucial, overly rigid communication can hinder innovation and problem-solving.
  - To mitigate this risk, it is important to balance the Directive Mode with elements of the Exploratory Mode, allowing for flexibility while maintaining overall structure. For instance, incorporating feedback mechanisms that enable adaptation and iterative improvement can help maintain effectiveness without stifling creativity or responsiveness.
- **Cultural Sensitivity and Communication Styles**:
  - The Directive Mode's emphasis on precision and structure may not always align with the communication styles of different cultures. In cross-cultural communication, it is important to adapt the Directive Mode to respect cultural norms and practices. This might involve modifying the level of directness or the way instructions are delivered to ensure they are received as intended (Hall, 1976).
  - Understanding these cultural differences is essential for

applying the Directive Mode effectively in a global context, particularly in international business or diplomacy. Adapting communication strategies to fit cultural expectations can enhance effectiveness and foster positive interactions.

- **Cognitive Overload**:
  - While the Directive Mode aims to reduce cognitive load, there is a risk that overly complex or dense information can overwhelm the receiver. This is particularly relevant in educational and AI contexts, where the goal is to simplify and clarify rather than complicate.
  - Effective application of the Directive Mode requires careful consideration of the audience's cognitive capacity and the complexity of the information being conveyed. Instructional design should focus on breaking down complex information into manageable parts to avoid overload. This approach can improve comprehension and ensure that the directive communication achieves its intended outcomes.

Future Research Directions and Open Questions

As the understanding and application of the Directive Mode continue to evolve, several areas offer potential for future research and development:

- **AI and Autonomous Systems**:
  - As AI systems become more autonomous, research into how the Directive Mode can be optimized within these systems will be crucial. This includes exploring how AI can dynamically adjust its communication strategies to maintain clarity in unpredictable environments. Future research might focus on developing AI algorithms that balance directive communication with the need for adaptability and user engagement (Gunning et al., 2019).
  - Additionally, the integration of ethical considerations into

directive AI systems, particularly in decision-making processes, will be an important area of exploration. Ensuring that AI systems can communicate their decisions transparently and ethically is critical for maintaining user trust and compliance with regulations.

- **Behavioral Economics and Public Policy**:

  - Further research into how the Directive Mode can be applied within the framework of behavioral economics could lead to more effective public policies. Understanding how structured communication influences decision-making at both the individual and societal levels can help policymakers design interventions that encourage positive behaviors while respecting autonomy (Thaler & Sunstein, 2008).
  - Investigating the long-term effects of nudges and directive communication on behavior change will provide valuable insights into the sustainability and impact of such approaches.

- **Cultural Adaptation of Directive Communication**:

  - Future research should also focus on the cultural adaptation of directive communication strategies. As global interactions become more prevalent, understanding how different cultures perceive and respond to directive communication will be essential for effective cross-cultural exchanges (Hall, 1976).
  - Studies could explore how to tailor directive communication to fit cultural contexts while maintaining its effectiveness in achieving desired outcomes. This includes examining the impact of cultural norms on the reception and interpretation of directive messages.

Conclusion

Chapter 2 has provided an in-depth exploration of the Directive Mode, highlighting its theoretical foundations, practical applications, and potential challenges. By integrating insights from cognitive psychology, behaviorism, linguistic theory, and evolutionary psychology, the Directive Mode emerges as a powerful framework for structured, goal-oriented communication. Its relevance across various fields—from education to AI—demonstrates its versatility and effectiveness in optimizing communication and decision-making. As research continues to advance, understanding and refining the Directive Mode will be crucial for addressing emerging challenges and harnessing its full potential in diverse contexts.

4.

The Exploratory Mode

Introduction

The Exploratory Mode within the Dual Mode Elicitation Model (DEM) is characterized by open-ended communication, creativity, and adaptability. Unlike the Directive Mode, which focuses on structured, goal-oriented communication, the Exploratory Mode embraces ambiguity and uncertainty, allowing for the exploration of new ideas and the adaptation to changing circumstances. This chapter delves into the theoretical foundations of the Exploratory Mode, examining its role in fostering creativity, innovation, and learning. Through an interdisciplinary lens, we will explore how insights from cognitive psychology, neuroscience, evolutionary psychology, and quantum decision theory contribute to the understanding and application of the Exploratory Mode.

Theoretical Foundations of the Exploratory Mode

The Exploratory Mode is grounded in several key theories that highlight the importance of flexibility, creativity, and adaptive thinking in communication and decision-making.

- **System 2 Processing (Kahneman, 2011):**
  - Daniel Kahneman's concept of System 2 processing, as outlined in *Thinking, Fast and Slow*, is central to the Exploratory Mode. System 2 is slow, deliberate, and analytical, engaging in deep processing and reflective thought to evaluate possibilities, weigh options, and consider multiple perspectives. This aligns with the Exploratory Mode's emphasis on intellectual curiosity, problem-solving, and adaptive thinking.
  - System 2 processing is particularly effective in complex

and ambiguous environments, where thorough analysis and strategic decision-making are necessary. In such contexts, the Exploratory Mode allows for careful hypothesis testing, deep questioning, and a tolerance for uncertainty, which are essential for scientific inquiry, philosophical reasoning, and innovation.

- **Reinforcement Learning (Sutton & Barto, 1998):**
    - Reinforcement learning, a type of machine learning where agents learn through trial and error, provides a framework for understanding how exploratory behavior is optimized. In the context of the Exploratory Mode, reinforcement learning emphasizes the importance of strategic experimentation, where individuals and groups actively seek out novel approaches, learn from past experiences, and refine their understanding over time.
    - This mirrors human learning, where trial-and-error exploration leads to creative breakthroughs and adaptive strategies. The Exploratory Mode encourages this type of cognitive expansion, allowing for innovation to emerge organically rather than through rigid adherence to predefined solutions.

- **Neuroscience of Creativity (Gazzaniga, 2000):**
    - Michael Gazzaniga's research on the neuroscience of creativity highlights the brain's ability to synthesize and integrate information across different neural networks. Creativity is often the result of slow, deliberate cross-pollination between seemingly unrelated concepts, a process that is central to the Exploratory Mode.
    - The prefrontal cortex, which governs executive function and higher-order reasoning, plays a critical role in the Exploratory Mode's depth-oriented, reflective nature. Unlike the automatic, reactive processes of System 1, the Exploratory Mode actively recruits deeper cognitive resources to generate insight. This is why environments

that promote mindful reflection and structured dialogue tend to enhance creativity and innovation.

Language, Social Learning, and the Exploratory Mode

The Exploratory Mode also draws from linguistic theory and social learning, emphasizing the role of language, metaphor, and cultural narratives in shaping adaptive communication strategies.

- **Language in Thought and Action (Hayakawa, 1949)**:
  - S.I. Hayakawa's Language in Thought and Action explores how language both reflects and constructs reality. In the Exploratory Mode, language is used as a cognitive tool for deconstructing assumptions, challenging existing beliefs, and constructing alternative viewpoints.
  - In practical terms, this means utilizing Socratic questioning, metaphor, and abstract reasoning to stimulate conceptual shifts and cognitive expansion. The Exploratory Mode encourages deep dialogue that fosters critical thinking rather than compliance, making it essential for academic discourse, psychotherapy, and strategic negotiations.
- **Social Learning Theory (Bandura, 1977)**:
  - Albert Bandura's social learning theory emphasizes the importance of observation and imitation in learning. The Exploratory Mode leverages collective intelligence by encouraging open dialogue, shared inquiry, and collaborative problem-solving.
  - In group settings, the Exploratory Mode facilitates reciprocal learning, where individuals build on each other's insights rather than simply absorbing information passively. This fosters intellectual autonomy, allowing for greater flexibility in thinking and decision-making.

Evolutionary Psychology and Exploratory Behavior

Exploratory behavior has deep roots in evolutionary psychology, where it is seen as a critical adaptation for survival and innovation.

- **Evolutionary Perspectives on Exploration (Cosmides & Tooby, 1992):**
  - From an evolutionary standpoint, humans have survived and thrived by engaging in exploratory behavior, testing the environment, and modifying their strategies based on feedback. This adaptive flexibility is a hallmark of the Exploratory Mode, which enables higher-order reasoning, abstract thinking, and adaptive innovation.
  - Rather than reacting automatically (System 1), the Exploratory Mode (System 2) allows individuals to pause, evaluate, and intentionally navigate complex environments, a skill crucial for scientific discovery, artistic creativity, and leadership.
- **Application in Innovation and Problem-Solving:**
  - In organizational settings, the Exploratory Mode is essential for fostering a culture of innovation. By encouraging employees to experiment, take risks, and learn from failures, organizations can develop new products, services, and strategies that give them a competitive edge. The Exploratory Mode thus plays a crucial role in driving innovation and continuous improvement.

Quantum Cognition and Decision Theory

Quantum cognition and decision theory provide a revolutionary perspective on how humans make decisions under uncertainty.

- **Quantum Decision Theory (Busemeyer & Bruza, 2012):**
  - Jerome Busemeyer's work on quantum decision theory suggests that human decision-making is not always linear and predictable. Instead, it follows probabilistic, non-

deterministic principles, meaning individuals entertain multiple mental states before resolving them into a concrete choice. The Exploratory Mode embraces this ambiguity, leveraging uncertainty as a source of creativity and insight. Instead of attempting to impose rigid structure, the Exploratory Mode thrives in environments where multiple perspectives and interpretations are explored before a decision is reached.

- **Implications for Adaptive Communication**:

  - Quantum cognition suggests that communication strategies should be flexible and adaptive, capable of accommodating multiple perspectives and potential outcomes. In practice, this means that the Exploratory Mode can be used to facilitate discussions that explore various possibilities and interpretations, leading to more nuanced and informed decisions.

Practical Applications of the Exploratory Mode

The Exploratory Mode is applied across a wide range of fields, each benefiting from its emphasis on creativity, adaptability, and open-ended exploration.

- **Education**:

  - In educational settings, the Exploratory Mode is essential for fostering critical thinking, creativity, and lifelong learning. It encourages students to engage with content in a deeper, more meaningful way, exploring different perspectives and developing their own interpretations. For example, in project-based learning environments, students are encouraged to explore real-world problems, collaborate with peers, and develop innovative solutions.

  - This approach contrasts with more traditional, directive forms of instruction by prioritizing the process of exploration and discovery over the mere acquisition of knowledge.

- **Artificial Intelligence and Machine Learning**:
  - In AI and machine learning, the Exploratory Mode is reflected in algorithms designed for exploration and innovation. Reinforcement learning, for example, relies on trial and error to discover effective strategies in dynamic environments. The Exploratory Mode can also inform the development of AI systems that generate creative outputs, such as art, music, or design, by simulating human-like exploratory behavior.
  - This mode is particularly important in the development of adaptive systems that must respond to changing environments or user preferences. By incorporating the principles of the Exploratory Mode, AI systems can become more flexible, responsive, and capable of innovation.
- **Therapy and Counseling**:
  - In therapeutic settings, the Exploratory Mode is used to help clients explore their thoughts, feelings, and behaviors in a safe and supportive environment. This mode encourages clients to reflect on their experiences, consider alternative perspectives, and experiment with new ways of thinking and behaving. Techniques such as open-ended questioning, narrative therapy, and mindfulness practices are all aligned with the Exploratory Mode.
  - The flexibility of the Exploratory Mode allows therapists to adapt their approach based on the client's needs, fostering a collaborative and dynamic therapeutic relationship.

Challenges and Limitations of the Exploratory Mode

While the Exploratory Mode offers significant benefits, it also presents certain challenges and limitations that must be managed to ensure effective communication and decision-making.

- **Risk of Ambiguity and Indecision**:

- One of the primary challenges of the Exploratory Mode is the risk of becoming lost in ambiguity or failing to reach a decisive conclusion. While exploration is valuable, it can sometimes lead to indecision or confusion if not carefully managed. In environments where timely decision-making is critical, this can be a significant drawback.
  - To mitigate this risk, it is important to balance the Exploratory Mode with the Directive Mode, ensuring that exploration is guided by clear goals and that decisions are ultimately reached based on the insights gained through exploration.

- **Overemphasis on Novelty**:
  - The Exploratory Mode's focus on creativity and novelty can sometimes lead to an overemphasis on new ideas at the expense of proven strategies. While innovation is important, it is also necessary to recognize the value of existing knowledge and practices. This balance is essential for maintaining both creativity and stability in decision-making and problem-solving.
  - Organizations and individuals must therefore be mindful of not discarding valuable traditions or strategies in the pursuit of novelty. A balanced approach that integrates exploration with the effective use of established knowledge is crucial for sustainable success.

Future Research Directions and Open Questions

As our understanding of the Exploratory Mode continues to evolve, several areas offer potential for future research and development:

- **Interdisciplinary Approaches to Exploration**:
  - Further research into the interdisciplinary applications of the Exploratory Mode could yield new insights into how different fields approach exploration and innovation. For example, examining how the principles of quantum

decision theory can be applied in organizational strategy or educational pedagogy could provide valuable perspectives on managing uncertainty and fostering creativity (Busemeyer & Bruza, 2012).

- Additionally, exploring the intersection of neuroscience and AI in the context of the Exploratory Mode could lead to the development of more adaptive and creative AI systems. This research could focus on how AI can simulate human-like exploratory behavior and the implications for human-AI collaboration.

- **Balancing Exploration and Exploitation**:

  - Future research should also investigate the balance between exploration and exploitation in various contexts. Understanding how to effectively balance these two approaches is crucial for optimizing decision-making, particularly in dynamic environments where both adaptability and efficiency are required.
  - Studies could explore how this balance is managed in different domains, from organizational leadership to personal development, and identify strategies for enhancing both exploratory and directive capacities.

- **Cultural Perspectives on Exploration**:

  - Research into cultural differences in exploratory behavior could provide valuable insights into how the Exploratory Mode is perceived and practiced in different contexts. Understanding these cultural variations can help tailor communication strategies to better fit diverse audiences and enhance cross-cultural collaboration.
  - Investigating how different cultures value exploration and creativity could also inform the development of educational programs, organizational policies, and global communication strategies that leverage the strengths of the Exploratory Mode.

Conclusion

Chapter 3 has provided a comprehensive exploration of the Exploratory Mode, highlighting its theoretical foundations, practical applications, and potential challenges. By integrating insights from cognitive psychology, neuroscience, linguistic theory, and quantum decision theory, the Exploratory Mode emerges as a powerful framework for fostering creativity, adaptability, and open-ended communication. Its relevance across various fields—from education to AI—demonstrates its versatility and importance in navigating the complexities of modern life. As research continues to advance, understanding and refining the Exploratory Mode will be crucial for addressing emerging challenges and harnessing its full potential in diverse contexts.

5.

The Dynamic Integration of Modes

Introduction

The Dual Mode Elicitation Model (DEM) is not merely a combination of directive and exploratory communication modes; it is a dynamic framework that seamlessly integrates these modes to optimize communication and decision-making across various contexts. This chapter delves into the techniques for integrating directive and exploratory modes within the DEM framework, drawing on a rich array of interdisciplinary research. By examining dual-process theories, deep learning, neural networks, cybernetics, and complex systems theory, we will explore how DEM can manage complex adaptive systems and adapt to diverse communication challenges. Case studies will illustrate successful implementations, providing practical insights into the dynamic integration of modes in real-world scenarios.

Theoretical Foundations of Dynamic Integration

Dynamic integration within DEM is grounded in several theoretical frameworks that explain how directive and exploratory modes can be effectively combined to enhance communication and decision-making.

- **Dual-Process Theories (Kahneman, 2011):**
  - Dual-process theories, such as those proposed by Daniel Kahneman in *Thinking, Fast and Slow*, provide the foundational understanding for integrating directive and exploratory modes. System 1 is fast, intuitive, and automatic, aligning with the Directive Mode of DEM, where quick, goal-oriented communication is necessary. System 2, on the other hand, is slow, deliberate, and

logical, reflecting the Exploratory Mode, which encourages open-ended communication and adaptability. Dynamic integration involves the seamless transition between these two systems, allowing for both quick, adaptive responses and careful, structured analysis as needed.

  - This integration is crucial for managing complex tasks that require both immediate action and long-term planning, ensuring that communication strategies are both flexible and precise.

- **Deep Learning and Neural Networks (LeCun, Bengio, & Hinton, 2015):**

  - Deep learning and neural networks offer insights into how complex systems can learn and adapt through the integration of different processing modes. Neural networks, particularly those involving deep learning architectures, are designed to process vast amounts of data and extract meaningful patterns. This is analogous to the dynamic integration in DEM, where directive and exploratory modes work together to process information and generate adaptive responses.

  - The layers of a neural network can be seen as representing different levels of processing, where earlier layers perform more exploratory, broad-based tasks, and deeper layers focus on more directive, goal-oriented tasks. This hierarchical approach supports the integration of both modes, ensuring that the system can handle both general and specific tasks effectively.

- **Cybernetic Principles and the Viable System Model (Wiener, 1948; Beer, 1972):**

  - Norbert Wiener's cybernetic principles and Stafford Beer's Viable System Model (VSM) provide a framework for understanding how systems can self-regulate and adapt through feedback loops. Cybernetics, the study of control and communication in animals and machines, emphasizes the importance of feedback in maintaining system stability and adaptability.

- The Viable System Model, developed by Beer, further elaborates on this by proposing that for a system to be viable, it must be capable of balancing stability with adaptability. In DEM, this balance is achieved by integrating directive and exploratory modes, where feedback mechanisms allow for continuous adjustment and optimization of communication strategies.
- This approach is particularly relevant in organizational settings, where dynamic integration ensures that strategic decisions are informed by both structured analysis and adaptive exploration, allowing the organization to remain resilient in the face of change.

Biological Basis of Adaptive Communication

The integration of directive and exploratory modes within DEM is also supported by biological principles, particularly those related to neural and behavioral adaptations.

- **Neural Plasticity and Adaptation (Kandel, 2006):**
  - Eric Kandel's research on neural plasticity highlights the brain's remarkable ability to adapt to new experiences and learn from them. Neural plasticity provides a biological basis for the dynamic integration of communication modes, as it allows the brain to switch between different cognitive strategies based on the demands of the situation.
  - In DEM, this adaptability is mirrored in the ability to transition between directive and exploratory modes. For example, in high-pressure situations, the brain may initially rely on the Exploratory Mode to gather information and assess the environment, before shifting to the Directive Mode to make a decisive, goal-oriented action.

- **Behavioral Adaptation and Evolutionary Perspectives (Cosmides & Tooby, 1992):**
  - From an evolutionary perspective, the ability to dynamically integrate different communication strategies has been crucial for survival. Behavioral adaptation, the process by which organisms adjust their behavior in response to environmental changes, is a key factor in the evolution of communication strategies.
  - The integration of directive and exploratory modes in DEM reflects this evolutionary need for adaptability. In complex, uncertain environments, the ability to switch between modes allows individuals and organizations to respond effectively to both immediate threats and long-term opportunities.
- **Embodied Cognition and Adaptive Communication (Gallagher, 2005):**
  - Embodied cognition, the theory that cognitive processes are deeply rooted in the body's interactions with the world, further supports the dynamic integration of modes. This perspective suggests that communication is not just a mental process but is also influenced by physical experiences and environmental contexts.
  - In DEM, embodied cognition plays a role in determining when to engage in directive or exploratory communication. For example, in face-to-face interactions, non-verbal cues such as body language can signal when to shift from a directive to an exploratory approach, ensuring that communication remains responsive and contextually appropriate.

Managing Complex Adaptive Systems

The dynamic integration of directive and exploratory modes is particularly valuable in managing complex adaptive systems, where multiple interconnected components interact in unpredictable ways.

- **Applications in Complex Systems (Holland, 1992):**
  - John H. Holland's work on complex adaptive systems provides insights into how systems composed of multiple interacting agents can adapt to changing environments. Complex systems are characterized by their ability to learn and evolve over time, often through the interaction of simple rules or behaviors.
  - In DEM, the integration of directive and exploratory modes allows for the management of such complexity by providing a framework for both structured decision-making and adaptive exploration. For example, in a corporate setting, dynamic integration can help an organization navigate market changes by combining strategic planning (Directive Mode) with innovative experimentation (Exploratory Mode).
- **Quantum Decision Theory (Busemeyer & Bruza, 2012):**
  - Quantum decision theory offers a novel perspective on decision-making in complex systems. Unlike classical decision theories that assume a linear, deterministic process, quantum decision theory suggests that decision-making can involve superposition and entanglement, where multiple potential outcomes are considered simultaneously.
  - The Exploratory Mode in DEM aligns with quantum decision theory by allowing for the consideration of multiple possibilities and the exploration of different pathways before committing to a decision. The Directive Mode then facilitates the transition from exploration to action, ensuring that decisions are implemented effectively.
- **Second-Order Cybernetics (von Foerster, 2003):**

- Heinz von Foerster's second-order cybernetics emphasizes the role of the observer in shaping the system they are studying. This perspective is particularly relevant in the context of DEM, where the communicator is both part of the communication process and an influencer of its outcomes.
  - In DEM, second-order cybernetics supports the dynamic integration of modes by recognizing that communication strategies must be continuously adjusted based on feedback and the evolving context. This approach is critical in complex systems where the relationships between components are constantly changing.

Techniques for Dynamic Integration in DEM

The dynamic integration of directive and exploratory modes within DEM requires specific techniques that enable the seamless transition between modes, ensuring that communication remains adaptive and effective.

- **Feedback Loops and Adaptive Learning:**
  - Feedback loops are essential for dynamic integration, as they provide the information needed to adjust communication strategies in real-time. In DEM, feedback loops can be used to monitor the effectiveness of both directive and exploratory communication, allowing for continuous improvement and adaptation.
  - Adaptive learning, where systems or individuals learn from their experiences and adjust their behavior accordingly, is another key technique. In educational settings, for example, dynamic integration can be achieved by using formative assessments (feedback) to guide the transition between directive instruction and exploratory learning activities.
- **Scenario Planning and Simulation:**
  - Scenario planning is a technique that allows organizations

to explore multiple potential futures and develop strategies that are robust across different scenarios. In DEM, scenario planning can be used to integrate directive and exploratory modes by outlining structured plans while also considering exploratory options for adaptation.

- Simulation, the process of creating a model of a real-world system that can be experimented with, is another valuable tool for dynamic integration. In AI development, simulations can be used to test how AI systems respond to different scenarios, ensuring that they can dynamically switch between directive and exploratory modes as needed.

- **Hybrid Systems and Algorithmic Integration**:

  - In the context of AI and machine learning, hybrid systems that combine rule-based (directive) and data-driven (exploratory) approaches can achieve dynamic integration. For example, an AI system might use a rule-based algorithm to handle routine tasks (Directive Mode) while employing machine learning to explore new patterns or behaviors (Exploratory Mode).

  - Algorithmic integration involves designing algorithms that can dynamically switch between directive and exploratory strategies based on the context. This approach is particularly relevant in adaptive systems that must respond to changing environments in real-time.

Case Studies: Dynamic Integration in Practice

To further illustrate the application of dynamic integration, this section presents several case studies from different fields.

- **Case Study 1: Blended Learning in Education**:

  - **Context**: A high school implements a blended learning environment where students alternate between directive online instruction and exploratory in-class activities. The goal is to create a seamless learning experience that leverages the strengths of both modes.

- **Application of Dynamic Integration**: In this blended learning model, students begin each week with online instructional modules that employ the Directive Mode. These modules provide clear, structured lessons that focus on key concepts and foundational knowledge. In the classroom, students then engage in exploratory projects that allow them to apply what they have learned in a more open-ended, creative manner. Teachers use formative assessments to provide feedback, guiding the transition between modes and ensuring that students remain engaged and motivated.

- **Outcomes**: The dynamic integration of directive and exploratory modes leads to improved student outcomes, including higher levels of engagement, deeper understanding of the material, and increased creativity. The flexibility of this approach allows students to take ownership of their learning while still benefiting from structured guidance.

- **Case Study 2: Integrative Therapy Approaches**:

  - **Context**: A therapy practice adopts an integrative approach that combines cognitive-behavioral therapy (CBT) with humanistic therapy. The aim is to provide a comprehensive treatment that addresses both the client's immediate concerns and their broader personal development.

  - **Application of Dynamic Integration**: In therapy sessions, the therapist uses CBT techniques (Directive Mode) to address specific issues such as anxiety or depression, providing structured guidance and actionable strategies. At the same time, the therapist incorporates humanistic approaches (Exploratory Mode) that encourage the client to explore their feelings, values, and goals in a more open-ended manner. This dynamic integration allows the therapist to adapt their approach based on the client's needs, creating a balanced therapeutic experience that promotes both healing and personal growth.

- ◦ **Outcomes**: Clients report higher levels of satisfaction with the therapy process, as they feel both supported and empowered to explore their own paths to recovery. The integration of directive and exploratory modes enhances the effectiveness of the therapy by addressing both immediate symptoms and underlying issues.

- **Case Study 3: Adaptive AI Systems in Customer Service**:

  - ◦ **Context**: A large e-commerce platform implements an AI-powered customer service system designed to handle a wide range of customer inquiries. The AI system must balance the need for quick, accurate responses with the ability to handle more complex, nuanced issues.

  - ◦ **Application of Dynamic Integration**: The AI system uses the Directive Mode to handle routine inquiries, such as order tracking and account management, providing clear and concise answers to customers. For more complex issues, such as product complaints or customization requests, the system switches to the Exploratory Mode, engaging the customer in a dialogue to better understand their needs and offer personalized solutions. The AI system is equipped with feedback loops that allow it to learn from each interaction and improve its responses over time.

  - ◦ **Outcomes**: The dynamic integration of directive and exploratory modes results in higher customer satisfaction and reduced need for human intervention. The AI system's ability to adapt its communication strategy based on the complexity of the inquiry ensures that customers receive the appropriate level of support, whether their needs are simple or complex.

Future Research Directions and Open Questions

As the understanding and application of dynamic integration in

DEM continue to evolve, several areas offer potential for future research and development:

- **Enhancing Hybrid AI Systems**:
    - Future research could explore how to enhance hybrid AI systems that dynamically integrate directive and exploratory modes. This includes developing algorithms that can better manage the transition between modes, ensuring that AI systems remain both efficient and adaptive in a wide range of contexts.
    - Additionally, research could focus on improving the feedback mechanisms within AI systems, allowing them to learn more effectively from their interactions and continuously refine their communication strategies.
- **Exploring Human-AI Collaboration**:
    - The dynamic integration of modes within DEM provides a valuable framework for improving human-AI collaboration. Future research could investigate how DEM can be applied to design AI systems that work more effectively alongside humans, balancing directive guidance with exploratory support to enhance teamwork and decision-making.
    - Studies could also explore how human-AI teams can dynamically integrate their respective strengths, such as human intuition and creativity with AI's processing power and precision, to solve complex problems.
- **Cultural and Contextual Adaptation**:
    - As DEM is applied in diverse cultural and contextual settings, research could focus on how to adapt the dynamic integration of modes to fit different environments. This might involve exploring how cultural norms and communication styles influence the effectiveness of directive and exploratory modes, and how these modes can be adjusted to enhance cross-cultural communication and collaboration.

- Further research could also examine how contextual factors, such as organizational culture or industry-specific challenges, impact the dynamic integration of modes and what strategies can be employed to optimize communication in these contexts.

Conclusion

Chapter 4 has provided an in-depth exploration of the dynamic integration of directive and exploratory modes within the Dual Mode Elicitation Model (DEM). By integrating insights from dual-process theories, deep learning, cybernetics, and complex systems theory, this chapter has highlighted how DEM can be applied to manage complex adaptive systems and enhance communication across various fields. The case studies have illustrated the practical application of dynamic integration, demonstrating its effectiveness in education, therapy, and AI systems. As research continues to advance, understanding and refining the dynamic integration of modes will be crucial for addressing emerging challenges and harnessing the full potential of DEM in diverse contexts.

6.

Applying DEM in AI Systems

Introduction

The application of the Dual Mode Elicitation Model (DEM) in artificial intelligence (AI) represents a significant advancement in the development of systems that simulate human communication and behavior. By integrating the principles of DEM with cutting-edge AI technologies, we can create systems that are not only capable of processing complex information but also of engaging in nuanced, adaptive communication. This chapter explores how DEM principles can be applied in AI development, focusing on the integration of neuromorphic computing, memristor technology, AI communication frameworks, human-computer interaction (HCI) research, neural adaptability, and embodied cognition. Through practical examples and case studies, we will examine the interdisciplinary contributions to AI and propose methodologies for testing and implementing DEM in AI systems.

Neuromorphic Computing and Memristor Technology

The integration of DEM in AI systems can be greatly enhanced by leveraging advancements in neuromorphic computing and memristor technology, which aim to mimic the biological processes of the human brain.

- **Neuromorphic Computing (Mead, 1990):**

    - Neuromorphic computing, pioneered by Carver Mead, involves the design of hardware and software systems that emulate the neural structures and processes of the human brain. These systems are characterized by their ability to process information in a parallel, distributed manner, similar to how the brain operates.

- In the context of DEM, neuromorphic computing provides a powerful platform for implementing both directive and exploratory modes of communication. By mimicking the brain's natural processing capabilities, neuromorphic systems can dynamically switch between structured, goal-oriented tasks and open-ended, exploratory problem-solving, depending on the demands of the situation.

- **Memristor Technology (HP Labs, 2008):**

  - Memristors, a type of non-volatile memory device, have the ability to store and process information simultaneously, much like synapses in the human brain. This technology is crucial for developing AI systems that require both memory retention and real-time adaptability.

  - When applied to DEM, memristor technology supports the integration of directive and exploratory modes by enabling AI systems to learn from past experiences while adapting to new inputs. This ability to balance memory with adaptability is essential for creating AI systems that can engage in complex, human-like communication.

AI Communication Frameworks

The application of DEM in AI requires the development of robust communication frameworks that can support both directive and exploratory modes.

- **AI Communication Frameworks:**

  - AI communication frameworks are designed to facilitate interactions between AI systems and human users. These frameworks must be capable of handling a wide range of communication tasks, from providing clear instructions to engaging in more nuanced, context-sensitive dialogues.

  - In DEM, AI communication frameworks must be able to switch seamlessly between directive and exploratory communication strategies. For example, an AI assistant might use the Directive Mode to provide clear, concise answers to user queries, while employing the Exploratory Mode to ask open-ended questions that encourage further discussion and exploration.

- These frameworks can be enhanced by incorporating natural language processing (NLP) technologies that allow AI systems to understand and generate human-like language. By integrating DEM principles with advanced NLP techniques, AI systems can achieve a higher level of responsiveness and adaptability in their interactions with users.

- **Human-Computer Interaction (HCI) Research (Shneiderman, 1980)**:

  - HCI research, as explored by Ben Shneiderman, focuses on optimizing the interaction between humans and computers to enhance usability and user experience. In the context of DEM, HCI principles are critical for designing AI systems that can effectively manage the transition between directive and exploratory communication modes.

  - For instance, HCI research can inform the design of user interfaces that support dynamic communication strategies, allowing users to seamlessly switch between receiving structured guidance and engaging in more open-ended exploration. This approach is particularly relevant in applications such as educational technology, where the ability to adapt to different learning styles is crucial.

Neural Adaptability and Embodied Cognition in AI

The integration of neural adaptability and embodied cognition into AI systems is essential for implementing DEM principles, as these concepts provide the foundation for creating AI that can adapt to changing environments and engage in human-like communication.

- **Neural Adaptability (Kandel, 2006)**:

- Neural adaptability, as discussed by Eric Kandel, refers to the brain's ability to reorganize itself in response to new experiences. This concept is directly applicable to AI systems that must adapt to changing inputs and contexts in real-time.
  - In DEM, neural adaptability enables AI systems to dynamically adjust their communication strategies based on user feedback and environmental changes. For example, an AI system that assists with medical diagnosis might start with a directive approach, providing clear recommendations based on established protocols. However, as the AI gathers more information about the patient's unique condition, it can switch to an exploratory approach, engaging in a more nuanced discussion with the healthcare provider to explore alternative diagnoses and treatments.

- **Embodied Cognition in AI (Gallagher, 2005):**
  - Embodied cognition posits that cognitive processes are deeply rooted in the physical interactions of the body with its environment. In AI, this means designing systems that can perceive and respond to physical and sensory inputs in a way that mimics human cognition.
  - Applying embodied cognition in DEM allows AI systems to engage in more natural and contextually aware communication. For instance, a robot designed for elder care might use the Directive Mode to provide instructions on medication adherence, while using the Exploratory Mode to engage in conversations about the patient's well-being, drawing on sensory data such as tone of voice and facial expressions to adapt its responses.
  - The integration of embodied cognition into AI systems also supports more immersive and interactive experiences, such as in virtual reality (VR) environments, where AI avatars can dynamically interact with users in ways that feel intuitive and responsive.

Case Studies: DEM in AI Systems

To better understand the practical application of DEM in AI systems, this section presents several case studies from different industries.

- **Case Study 1: Virtual Healthcare Assistant:**
  - **Context**: A healthcare provider develops a virtual healthcare assistant (VHA) to support patients with chronic conditions. The AI system is designed to assist with medication management, symptom monitoring, and lifestyle recommendations.
  - **Application of DEM**: The VHA uses the Directive Mode to provide clear instructions on daily medication routines, ensuring patients follow their prescribed treatment plans. During consultations, the VHA switches to the Exploratory Mode to discuss the patient's lifestyle choices, preferences, and concerns. This approach allows the AI to offer personalized advice and engage the patient in a deeper dialogue about their health.
  - **Outcomes**: The integration of DEM principles enhances patient engagement and adherence to treatment plans, resulting in improved health outcomes. The VHA's ability to adapt its communication strategy based on the patient's responses fosters a more personalized and supportive healthcare experience.

- **Case Study 2: AI-Powered Financial Advisor:**
  - **Context**: A financial services company develops an AI-powered financial advisor to help users manage their investments and make informed financial decisions.
  - **Application of DEM**: The AI advisor uses the Directive Mode to provide specific investment recommendations based on the user's financial goals and risk tolerance. When users seek more information or express uncertainty,

the system switches to the Exploratory Mode, engaging the user in a dialogue to discuss alternative investment strategies, explain the potential risks and rewards, and address any concerns the user may have.

- **Outcomes**: The dynamic integration of directive and exploratory modes results in a more personalized financial planning experience. Users feel more confident and informed about their investment choices, leading to higher satisfaction and better financial outcomes. The AI's ability to adapt its communication approach based on the user's preferences and needs fosters trust and encourages continued engagement with the platform.

- **Case Study 3: Customer Service AI for E-Commerce**:

  - **Context**: A large e-commerce platform implements an AI-driven customer service system designed to handle a wide range of customer inquiries, from order tracking to complex product support issues.

  - **Application of DEM**: The AI system initially employs the Directive Mode to guide customers through common tasks such as checking order status or initiating returns, using clear, straightforward language. For more complex or personalized queries, such as product recommendations or troubleshooting issues, the system transitions to the Exploratory Mode. Here, the AI engages in a more detailed conversation to understand the customer's specific needs and provide tailored solutions.

  - **Outcomes**: The use of DEM principles in the customer service AI leads to improved user satisfaction by efficiently addressing routine inquiries while also offering personalized assistance for more complex issues. The system's ability to switch between modes based on the complexity of the inquiry reduces the need for human intervention, streamlines operations, and enhances the overall customer experience.

Methodologies for Testing and Implementing DEM in AI Systems

To ensure the successful application of DEM in AI systems, it is essential to develop and implement rigorous methodologies for testing and evaluation. These methodologies should assess the AI system's ability to effectively integrate directive and exploratory modes and adapt to various communication contexts.

- **Performance Metrics and Evaluation:**
  - Developing appropriate performance metrics is crucial for evaluating the effectiveness of DEM integration in AI systems. Metrics might include user satisfaction, response accuracy, adaptability to new information, and the system's ability to maintain engagement in exploratory dialogues. Regularly monitoring these metrics can help identify areas for improvement and ensure that the AI system continues to perform effectively across different scenarios.
  - A/B testing can be employed to compare the performance of AI systems with and without DEM integration. By analyzing user interactions and outcomes in controlled experiments, developers can gain insights into the impact of dynamic integration on communication effectiveness and user experience.
- **Simulation and Iterative Development:**
  - Simulation environments can be used to test AI systems under various scenarios, allowing developers to observe how well the system transitions between directive and exploratory modes in different contexts. This approach is particularly useful for fine-tuning AI behavior before deploying it in real-world applications.
  - An iterative development process, involving regular updates and refinements based on user feedback and performance data, is essential for maintaining the effectiveness of DEM integration. This approach ensures

that the AI system evolves in response to changing user needs and technological advancements.

- **Ethical Considerations and User Privacy**:

  - Implementing DEM in AI systems also raises important ethical considerations, particularly related to user privacy and data security. It is essential to ensure that AI systems using DEM principles adhere to strict ethical standards, protecting user data while providing personalized and adaptive communication.

  - Developers should consider how the AI system's ability to engage in exploratory dialogue might impact user trust and autonomy. Transparent communication about how the system uses data to personalize interactions can help mitigate concerns and foster a more positive user experience.

Future Research Directions and Open Questions

As the integration of DEM into AI systems continues to evolve, several areas offer promising avenues for future research and development:

- **Advanced Neuromorphic Architectures**:

  - Future research could explore the development of more advanced neuromorphic architectures that better simulate the dynamic integration of directive and exploratory modes in AI systems. This could involve designing new types of neural networks that are specifically optimized for switching between different cognitive strategies based on real-time inputs and contextual cues.

- **Human-AI Collaboration and Hybrid Systems**:

  - The potential for DEM to enhance human-AI collaboration presents an exciting area for future research. Studies could focus on how AI systems that integrate DEM principles can work alongside humans in complex decision-making processes, leveraging the strengths of both human intuition and machine precision.

- Hybrid systems that combine human expertise with AI's adaptive communication capabilities could be particularly valuable in fields such as healthcare, education, and strategic planning, where the balance of directive guidance and exploratory dialogue is crucial.

- **Impact of Embodied Cognition on AI Communication:**

  - Further research into the role of embodied cognition in AI communication could provide insights into how physical and sensory inputs can enhance the AI's ability to engage in more natural and contextually appropriate interactions. This could lead to the development of AI systems that are better able to understand and respond to human emotions, body language, and environmental factors.

- **Ethical Implications and Bias in AI Communication:**

  - As AI systems become more adept at integrating directive and exploratory modes, it will be important to explore the ethical implications of this capability. Research could focus on how to mitigate the risk of bias in AI communication, ensuring that the system's adaptability does not lead to unintended consequences or discriminatory behavior.

  - Additionally, studies could investigate the long-term impact of AI systems that use DEM principles on user autonomy and decision-making, exploring how these systems influence human behavior and the potential for both positive and negative outcomes.

Conclusion

Chapter 5 has provided a comprehensive exploration of how the Dual Mode Elicitation Model (DEM) can be applied in AI systems to enhance communication and behavior simulation. By integrating principles from neuromorphic computing, memristor technology, AI communication frameworks, and embodied cognition, AI systems can achieve a higher level of responsiveness and adaptability. The case studies presented in this chapter illustrate the practical applications of DEM in various industries, demonstrating its potential to improve user experience and decision-making. As research and technology continue to advance, the ongoing refinement and implementation of DEM in AI systems will be crucial for realizing the full potential of this innovative approach.

7.

Introduction to Signature-based AI

Introduction

Signature-based AI represents a transformative approach in artificial intelligence, focusing on the replication and adaptation of human personalities to create more personalized and responsive systems. This chapter introduces the concept of Signature-based AI, emphasizing the role of the Dual Mode Elicitation Model (DEM) in developing these systems. By integrating insights from psycholinguistics, cognitive psychology, neural adaptability, behavioral genetics, computational psychometrics, and explainable AI (XAI), we explore how Signature-based AI can be used to enhance human-computer interactions. This chapter will also address potential research opportunities and ethical considerations associated with this emerging technology.

Defining Signature-Based AI

Signature-based AI refers to AI systems designed to replicate and adapt human personalities by mapping individual personality traits and preferences to create a "signature" that guides the system's interactions. This approach allows AI to provide more personalized and contextually appropriate responses, enhancing the user experience.

- **Personality Mapping and Insight Modeling**:
  - Personality mapping involves identifying and encoding individual personality traits, preferences, and behaviors into a model that the AI system can use to simulate human-like interactions. Insight modeling builds on this by enabling the AI to predict and adapt to the user's needs, preferences, and emotional states.

- The integration of DEM into Signature-based AI allows for the dynamic application of directive and exploratory communication modes based on the user's personality signature. This capability is particularly valuable in applications such as virtual assistants, customer service bots, and educational platforms, where personalized interactions can significantly enhance user satisfaction and engagement.

- **Role of DEM in Signature-Based AI:**

  - DEM facilitates the creation of adaptive AI systems by providing a framework for balancing structured, goal-oriented communication with open-ended, exploratory dialogue. In Signature-based AI, this balance is crucial for replicating the nuances of human communication and adapting to the evolving needs of the user.

  - For example, an AI system might use the Directive Mode to offer clear, concise instructions when interacting with a user who prefers structured guidance. Conversely, it might employ the Exploratory Mode to engage in more flexible, adaptive conversations with a user who values creativity and exploration.

Psycholinguistics and Cognitive Psychology in Signature-Based AI

The development of Signature-based AI is deeply rooted in the principles of psycholinguistics and cognitive psychology, which provide insights into how language and thought interact to shape human communication.

- **Psycholinguistics (Chomsky, 1957; Pinker, 1994):**

  - Noam Chomsky's theories on the innate structures of language and Steven Pinker's work on the language instinct underscore the importance of understanding the cognitive mechanisms underlying language use. In Signature-based AI, psycholinguistic models help the AI system understand and replicate the intricacies of human language, enabling it to generate responses that align with the user's communication style.

  - For instance, by analyzing a user's language patterns, the AI can identify whether they prefer formal or informal language, direct or indirect communication, and adjust its responses accordingly. This alignment enhances the naturalness and effectiveness of AI interactions, making them more personalized and engaging.

- **Cognitive Psychology and Personality**:

  - Cognitive psychology provides a framework for understanding how personality influences thought processes, decision-making, and communication styles. The integration of cognitive psychology into Signature-based AI allows the system to model and predict user behavior based on their cognitive traits, such as their tendency towards analytical thinking or intuition.

  - By incorporating cognitive psychological principles, Signature-based AI can adapt its communication strategy to better match the user's cognitive style. For example, an AI system might offer more detailed, analytical explanations to a user who prefers logical reasoning, while providing intuitive, big-picture insights to a user who favors holistic thinking.

Neural Adaptability and Behavioral Genetics in Personalized AI

The adaptability of AI systems to individual users is a key component of Signature-based AI, supported by concepts from neural adaptability and behavioral genetics.

- **Neural Adaptability (Kandel, 2006):**

  - As discussed by Eric Kandel, neural adaptability refers to the brain's ability to reorganize itself in response to new experiences. In Signature-based AI, neural adaptability is mirrored by the system's ability to learn from user interactions and adjust its behavior accordingly.

- For example, an AI system might start with a basic personality model and refine it over time as it gathers more data about the user's preferences and behaviors. This ongoing adaptation ensures that the AI remains responsive to the user's evolving needs, providing a more personalized and effective experience.

- **Behavioral Genetics and Personalized Communication Strategies**:

  - Behavioral genetics explores how genetic factors influence individual differences in behavior, personality, and cognition. In the context of Signature-based AI, understanding these genetic influences can inform the development of personalized communication strategies that are tailored to the user's innate traits.

  - For instance, if research indicates that certain genetic markers are associated with a preference for structured environments, an AI system could use this information to tailor its communication strategy for users with those markers. This approach not only enhances personalization but also opens up new avenues for integrating biological data into AI systems.

Computational Psychometrics and Explainable AI (XAI)

The success of Signature-based AI relies heavily on computational psychometrics and explainable AI, which provide the tools needed to accurately model and communicate human personalities.

- **Computational Psychometrics (Kosinski, Stillwell, & Graepel, 2013)**:

  - Computational psychometrics involves the use of algorithms to assess and predict psychological traits based on digital footprints, such as social media activity, browsing history, and communication patterns. In Signature-based AI, these techniques are used to create detailed personality profiles that guide the AI's interactions.

- ○ For example, by analyzing a user's online behavior, the AI can infer their openness to new experiences, conscientiousness, and other personality traits. This information allows the AI to tailor its responses to better align with the user's preferences, creating a more personalized and engaging experience.

- **Explainable AI (XAI) (Gunning, Doshi-Velez, & Kim, 2017):**

  - ○ Explainable AI is critical for ensuring that the decisions and behaviors of Signature-based AI systems are transparent and understandable to users. XAI techniques allow AI systems to articulate the reasoning behind their actions, making them more trustworthy and easier to interact with.

  - ○ In Signature-based AI, XAI plays a crucial role in helping users understand how the AI's personality model was developed and how it informs the system's responses. This transparency is essential for building user trust, particularly in applications where AI decisions have significant personal or ethical implications.

Ethical Considerations in Signature-Based AI

As with any advanced technology, the development of Signature-based AI raises important ethical considerations, particularly related to privacy, consent, and the potential for bias.

- **Privacy and Data Security:**

  - ○ The creation of detailed personality profiles requires the collection and analysis of large amounts of personal data, raising concerns about privacy and data security. Ensuring that users have control over their data and understand how it is being used is critical for maintaining trust in Signature-based AI systems.

  - ○ Developers must implement robust security measures to protect user data from unauthorized access and ensure that data collection and processing practices comply with relevant privacy regulations.

- **Bias and Fairness**:
    - The algorithms used in Signature-based AI are only as fair and unbiased as the data they are trained on. There is a risk that these systems could inadvertently reinforce existing biases, leading to unfair or discriminatory outcomes.
    - To mitigate this risk, it is essential to develop and implement fairness-aware algorithms that actively work to identify and counteract potential biases in the data. This may involve using diverse and representative training datasets, as well as regularly auditing AI systems to ensure they are not perpetuating harmful biases.
- **Autonomy and Consent**:
    - Signature-based AI has the potential to influence user behavior in subtle ways, raising questions about autonomy and consent. Users must be informed about how the AI system is using their data to influence interactions and given the opportunity to opt out of certain features if they wish.
    - Additionally, AI systems should be designed to enhance, rather than diminish, user autonomy. This could involve providing users with greater control over the AI's behavior or offering multiple interaction modes that cater to different levels of user involvement.

Future Research Directions and Open Questions

The field of Signature-based AI is still in its early stages, with many opportunities for future research and development.

- **Advanced Personality Modeling Techniques**:
    - Future research could focus on developing more sophisticated techniques for personality modeling,

incorporating insights from neuropsychology, behavioral genetics, and computational psychometrics. These models could be used to create even more accurate and dynamic personality profiles, enhancing the personalization capabilities of AI systems.

  ◦ Additionally, research could explore how to integrate real-time feedback into personality models, allowing AI systems to continuously update and refine their understanding of the user.

- **Cross-Cultural Considerations in Signature-Based AI:**

  ◦ As Signature-based AI systems are deployed globally, it is important to consider how cultural differences may impact personality modeling and communication strategies. Research could investigate how to adapt AI systems to different cultural contexts, ensuring that they remain effective and respectful across diverse populations.

  ◦ This research could also explore the role of cultural norms in shaping communication preferences, and how AI systems can be designed to navigate these complexities.

- **Ethical Frameworks for Personalized AI:**

  ◦ Developing comprehensive ethical frameworks for Signature-based AI is crucial for ensuring that these systems are used responsibly. Future research could focus on creating guidelines for the ethical design, implementation, and regulation of personalized AI, addressing issues such as privacy, consent, and bias.

  ◦ These frameworks could also explore the broader societal implications of Signature-based AI, including its impact on human relationships, decision-making, and autonomy.

Conclusion

Chapter 6 has introduced Signature-based AI, highlighting its potential to revolutionize human-computer interactions by replicating and adapting human personalities. By integrating principles from psycholinguistics, cognitive psychology, neural adaptability, behavioral genetics, computational psychometrics, and explainable AI, Signature-based AI systems can offer highly personalized and responsive communication experiences. However, the development of these systems also raises important ethical considerations, particularly related to privacy, bias, and autonomy. As research and technology continue to advance, the ongoing refinement of Signature-based AI will be crucial for ensuring that these systems are both effective and ethical.

8.

Developing Empathetic AI with DEM

Introduction

Empathy is a cornerstone of effective human communication, playing a crucial role in understanding others' emotions and responding appropriately. As artificial intelligence (AI) systems become more integrated into our daily lives, the ability to simulate empathy has become increasingly important. This chapter explores the development of empathetic AI systems using the Dual Mode Elicitation Model (DEM), focusing on how to balance directive and exploratory modes to create responsive, emotionally intelligent systems. By integrating insights from cognitive neuroscience, AI ethics, emotional intelligence research, and Artificial Emotional Intelligence (AEI), this chapter provides a comprehensive guide to developing AI systems that can understand and respond to human emotions effectively.

Understanding Empathy in AI

Empathy in AI refers to the system's ability to recognize, understand, and respond to human emotions in a way that mimics human empathetic behavior. This capability is essential for creating AI systems that can engage in meaningful interactions with users, particularly in sensitive contexts such as healthcare, customer service, and education.

- **Cognitive Neuroscience of Empathy (Decety & Jackson, 2004):**

  - Cognitive neuroscience provides the foundation for understanding how empathy is processed in the human brain. Studies have shown that empathy involves the activation of specific neural networks associated with emotional processing and perspective-taking. These insights are critical for developing AI systems that can simulate empathy, as they inform the design of algorithms that mimic these neural processes.

- ○ For instance, by modeling the neural mechanisms underlying empathy, AI systems can be designed to recognize emotional cues such as facial expressions, tone of voice, and language patterns, allowing them to respond in ways that are contextually appropriate and emotionally supportive.

- **Artificial Emotional Intelligence (AEI) (Zeng et al., 2009; Picard, 1997):**

  - ○ Artificial Emotional Intelligence (AEI) refers to the capability of AI systems to recognize and respond to human emotions. AEI involves the integration of affective computing technologies, which enable AI to detect and interpret emotional signals from users.

  - ○ In the context of DEM, AEI can be used to balance directive and exploratory communication modes based on the user's emotional state. For example, an AI system might use the Directive Mode to provide clear guidance when a user is anxious or stressed, while switching to the Exploratory Mode to engage in a more supportive, open-ended dialogue when the user is experiencing complex emotions.

Balancing Directive and Exploratory Modes in Empathetic AI

The Dual Mode Elicitation Model (DEM) provides a framework for integrating empathy into AI systems by balancing structured, goal-oriented responses with flexible, emotionally intelligent interactions.

- **Directive Mode for Structured Emotional Support:**

  - ○ In situations where users need clear, direct guidance, such as during a crisis or when making important decisions, the Directive Mode can be employed to provide structured emotional support. This might involve offering step-by-step instructions, providing reassurance, or delivering factual information in a calm and controlled manner.

- For example, in a healthcare context, an empathetic AI system might use the Directive Mode to guide a patient through their treatment options, providing clear explanations and addressing concerns in a straightforward manner. This approach helps to reduce anxiety and build trust, particularly in high-stress situations.

- **Exploratory Mode for Emotional Exploration and Understanding:**

  - The Exploratory Mode is essential for situations that require a deeper understanding of the user's emotions, such as during counseling sessions or when dealing with complex interpersonal issues. This mode allows the AI to engage in open-ended conversations, encouraging users to express their feelings and explore their emotions in a safe and supportive environment.

  - In an educational setting, for example, an empathetic AI tutor might use the Exploratory Mode to help a student work through their frustration or confusion about a difficult subject, asking open-ended questions and providing encouragement as the student articulates their thoughts and emotions.

Techniques for Developing Empathetic AI Systems

Developing AI systems that can effectively simulate empathy requires the integration of various techniques and technologies, guided by DEM principles.

- **Emotion Recognition and Interpretation:**

  - Emotion recognition technologies enable AI systems to detect and interpret emotional signals from users, such as facial expressions, voice tone, and physiological responses. These technologies are critical for empathetic AI, as they provide the data needed to adjust the system's communication strategy in real-time.

- ◦ For instance, if an AI system detects signs of stress or frustration in a user's voice, it might switch from a directive to an exploratory approach, offering the user an opportunity to discuss their feelings and providing support.

- **Natural Language Processing (NLP) for Empathy Simulation**:

  - ◦ Natural Language Processing (NLP) techniques are essential for enabling AI systems to engage in empathetic conversations. By analyzing the language used by the user, the AI can infer their emotional state and respond in a way that is contextually appropriate and emotionally supportive.
  - ◦ For example, an AI-powered customer service bot might use NLP to detect when a customer is upset and respond with a more empathetic tone, offering apologies and solutions that acknowledge the customer's emotional state.

- **Affective Computing and Adaptive Feedback**:

  - ◦ Affective computing involves the development of systems that can recognize, interpret, and simulate human emotions. In empathetic AI, affective computing technologies can be used to provide adaptive feedback based on the user's emotional responses.
  - ◦ For instance, in a therapy setting, an AI counselor might use affective computing to monitor the patient's emotional state throughout the session, adjusting its approach based on real-time feedback. If the patient becomes distressed, the AI might shift to a more comforting and supportive mode, offering reassurance and empathy.

Practical Applications of Empathetic AI

Empathetic AI has a wide range of applications across different industries, each benefiting from the system's ability to balance directive and exploratory modes to provide emotionally intelligent interactions.

- **Healthcare and Mental Health**:
  - In healthcare, empathetic AI systems can provide support to patients by recognizing their emotional states and responding with appropriate empathy. For instance, an AI system might assist in managing chronic conditions by offering both medical advice (Directive Mode) and emotional support (Exploratory Mode), helping patients navigate the psychological challenges of their illness.
  - In mental health, empathetic AI can be used in virtual therapy sessions, where the system provides real-time emotional support and helps users explore their feelings. By integrating DEM, these systems can adapt their approach based on the patient's needs, switching between structured therapeutic techniques and open-ended exploration.
- **Customer Service and User Support**:
  - Empathetic AI systems in customer service can enhance the user experience by recognizing and responding to the emotional states of customers. For example, if a customer is frustrated with a product issue, the AI can use the Directive Mode to provide clear instructions on resolving the problem, while also using the Exploratory Mode to offer empathetic listening and personalized solutions.
  - These systems can also improve customer loyalty by creating a more human-like interaction, where customers feel understood and valued.
- **Education and Tutoring**:
  - In educational settings, empathetic AI tutors can provide personalized learning experiences by adapting to the emotional needs of students. For example, an AI tutor

might detect when a student is struggling with a particular topic and switch to the Exploratory Mode, offering encouragement and alternative explanations to help the student understand the material.

- By balancing directive instruction with emotional support, empathetic AI tutors can help students build confidence and achieve better learning outcomes.

Ethical Considerations in Empathetic AI

The development and deployment of empathetic AI systems raise significant ethical questions, particularly regarding privacy, bias, and the potential manipulation of emotions.

- **Privacy and Emotional Data:**
  - Empathetic AI systems rely on the collection and analysis of sensitive emotional data, raising concerns about privacy and data security. It is crucial to ensure that users have control over their emotional data and that it is stored and processed securely.
  - Transparent communication about how emotional data is used and the implementation of robust data protection measures are essential for maintaining user trust.
- **Bias in Emotion Recognition:**
  - Emotion recognition technologies can be susceptible to bias, particularly if they are trained on non-representative data. This bias can lead to inaccuracies in detecting and interpreting emotions, which can result in inappropriate or harmful responses from the AI.
  - Developers must be vigilant in ensuring that emotion recognition systems are trained on diverse datasets and regularly audited to identify and correct biases.
- **Manipulation and User Autonomy:**
  - Empathetic AI systems have the potential to manipulate users by exploiting their emotions, raising concerns about

user autonomy. It is important to design AI systems that prioritize user well-being and autonomy, avoiding manipulative practices that could undermine trust and agency.

- Ethical guidelines and regulatory frameworks should be established to ensure that empathetic AI is used responsibly, with a focus on enhancing, rather than exploiting, user emotions.

Future Research Directions and Open Questions

The field of empathetic AI is rapidly evolving, with many opportunities for future research and development.

- **Advancements in Emotion Recognition and Simulation:**
  - Future research could focus on improving the accuracy and reliability of emotion recognition technologies, particularly in understanding subtle or complex emotional states. Advancements in affective computing and machine learning could lead to more sophisticated AI systems that can simulate empathy more effectively.
  - Additionally, research could explore how AI systems can better simulate and express empathy through non-verbal communication, such as facial expressions, gestures, and tone of voice.
- **Cross-Cultural Empathy in AI:**
  - As empathetic AI systems are deployed globally, it is important to consider how cultural differences in emotional expression and empathy are addressed. Research could investigate how AI systems can be adapted to recognize and respond to emotions in ways that are culturally appropriate and respectful.
  - This research could also explore the role of cultural norms in shaping emotional communication and how AI systems can navigate these complexities to provide effective and empathetic interactions.

- **Ethical Frameworks for Empathetic AI**:
    - Developing comprehensive ethical frameworks for empathetic AI is essential for ensuring that these systems are used responsibly. Future research could focus on creating guidelines for the ethical design, implementation, and regulation of empathetic AI, addressing issues such as privacy, bias, and the potential for emotional manipulation.
    - These frameworks could also explore the broader societal implications of empathetic AI, including its impact on human relationships, trust, and autonomy.

Conclusion

Chapter 7 has provided a comprehensive exploration of developing empathetic AI systems using the Dual Mode Elicitation Model (DEM). By integrating insights from cognitive neuroscience, AI ethics, emotional intelligence research, and Artificial Emotional Intelligence (AEI), this chapter has outlined techniques for creating AI systems that balance directive and exploratory modes to provide emotionally intelligent interactions. The practical applications and ethical considerations discussed in this chapter highlight the potential and challenges of empathetic AI, emphasizing the need for ongoing research and responsible development. As AI continues to evolve, the ability to simulate empathy will be crucial for creating systems that enhance, rather than diminish, human well-being.

9.

Future Applications of DEM in AI

Introduction

The Dual Mode Elicitation Model (DEM) represents a versatile framework with vast potential to shape the future of artificial intelligence (AI). As AI continues to evolve, DEM's ability to integrate directive and exploratory modes of communication positions it as a cornerstone for developing advanced AI systems that are adaptive, responsive, and capable of simulating complex human behaviors. This chapter explores speculative future applications of DEM in AI, focusing on Digital Continuance Profiles, self-determining AI systems, and the integration of cutting-edge technologies such as neuromemristive systems, VR/AR, and quantum decision theory. We will also address the ethical considerations of autonomous decision-making and the long-term impacts of these innovations on society.

Future Trends in AI and the Role of DEM

To understand the potential future applications of DEM in AI, it is essential to first explore the overarching trends that are likely to shape AI development in the coming decades.

- **AI's Increasing Role in Daily Life**:
  - AI systems are becoming increasingly embedded in various aspects of daily life, from smart home devices and personal assistants to advanced medical diagnostics and financial management tools. As these systems grow more sophisticated, the need for AI that can engage in nuanced, adaptive communication will become more critical. DEM provides the necessary framework for developing AI systems that can navigate complex social interactions and

respond to human emotions and intentions effectively.

- ◦ As AI systems become more integrated into society, their ability to seamlessly switch between directive and exploratory modes will be crucial for maintaining user trust and ensuring that these systems can handle both routine tasks and unexpected challenges with equal competence.

- **Advances in Human-AI Interaction**:

  - ◦ Future AI systems will increasingly focus on enhancing human-AI interaction, making it more natural, intuitive, and emotionally resonant. The DEM framework can guide the development of AI systems that can interpret and respond to a wide range of human communication styles, preferences, and emotional states, ensuring that interactions remain fluid and meaningful.
  - ◦ This trend will be particularly important in the context of AI-driven customer service, healthcare, and education, where the ability to engage in empathetic and contextually appropriate communication will set apart the most successful AI systems.

Digital Continuance Profiles

One of the most intriguing future applications of DEM in AI is the creation of Digital Continuance Profiles—AI-generated representations that preserve and extend an individual's personality, knowledge, and communication style.

- **Concept and Potential Applications**:

  - ◦ Digital Continuance Profiles (DCPs) are AI systems designed to replicate an individual's personality, preferences, and decision-making patterns, allowing their digital presence to continue even after they are no longer actively involved. These profiles could be used in various contexts, including legacy management, where a person's digital profile could manage their online presence, provide guidance to family members, or even participate in ongoing projects based on the individual's known preferences and values.

  ◦ In the professional realm, DCPs could serve as virtual consultants or mentors, providing continuity in leadership or expertise by simulating the decision-making processes and communication styles of key individuals.

- **Integration with DEM:**

  ◦ DEM is integral to the development of DCPs, as it allows these profiles to dynamically adjust their communication strategies based on the context and the needs of the users they interact with. For example, a DCP might use the Directive Mode to provide clear, actionable advice on business decisions while employing the Exploratory Mode to engage in more reflective, open-ended discussions about personal or philosophical matters.

  ◦ The ability to switch between these modes ensures that DCPs remain flexible and responsive, capable of handling a wide range of scenarios in a manner consistent with the individual's established personality and communication style.

Self-Determining AI Systems

Another significant future application of DEM is in the development of self-determining AI systems—AI entities that possess the capability to make autonomous decisions, set their goals, and adapt to complex environments without direct human intervention.

- **Defining Self-Determining AI:**

  ◦ Self-determining AI systems are envisioned as AI entities that not only perform tasks independently but also possess the ability to define their objectives, learn from their environments, and evolve over time. These systems would operate with a degree of autonomy that goes beyond current AI capabilities, potentially leading to the development of AI entities that could participate in decision-making processes at levels comparable to or even surpassing human counterparts.

  - The concept of self-determining AI raises profound questions about the nature of autonomy, intelligence, and the role of AI in society. It also introduces new challenges related to control, accountability, and ethics, particularly in scenarios where AI systems might make decisions with significant moral or societal implications.

- **Role of DEM in Self-Determining AI:**

  - DEM provides the foundational structure for self-determining AI by enabling these systems to balance structured decision-making (Directive Mode) with the ability to explore new possibilities and adapt to changing circumstances (Exploratory Mode). This dynamic integration is crucial for creating AI systems that can operate autonomously in complex, unpredictable environments.

  - For instance, in a scenario where a self-determining AI is tasked with managing a large-scale environmental project, it might use the Directive Mode to implement established conservation strategies while employing the Exploratory Mode to investigate new methods or respond to unforeseen challenges. This flexibility ensures that the AI system remains effective and resilient, capable of achieving its objectives even in the face of uncertainty.

Integration with Emerging Technologies

The future of DEM in AI will likely involve its integration with several emerging technologies, including virtual and augmented reality (VR/AR), neuromemristive systems, and quantum decision theory.

- **VR/AR Integration:**

- Virtual and augmented reality technologies are transforming the way we interact with digital environments. Integrating DEM into VR/AR systems could enhance these experiences by enabling AI-driven avatars and environments to respond more naturally and adaptively to users' actions and emotions.
- In a VR training simulation, for example, an AI instructor could use the Directive Mode to guide the user through specific tasks, while switching to the Exploratory Mode to allow for more creative problem-solving and experimentation. This adaptability could make VR/AR applications more immersive and effective, particularly in fields such as education, healthcare, and entertainment.

- **Neuromemristive Systems**:

  - Neuromemristive systems, which combine neural and memristive technologies to mimic the brain's ability to learn and adapt, represent a promising avenue for implementing DEM in future AI systems. These systems could provide the hardware support needed for AI to process and integrate information dynamically, switching between directive and exploratory modes as needed.
  - For example, in a neuromemristive AI designed for autonomous vehicles, DEM could enable the system to make split-second decisions using the Directive Mode during normal driving conditions, while engaging the Exploratory Mode to assess and respond to unexpected road hazards or changes in traffic patterns.

- **Quantum Decision Theory (Busemeyer & Bruza, 2012)**:

  - Quantum decision theory offers a novel approach to decision-making that accounts for the probabilistic and non-linear nature of human cognition. Integrating quantum decision theory with DEM could lead to the development of AI systems capable of handling complex, ambiguous situations with greater flexibility and precision.

- In financial markets, for example, an AI system using quantum decision theory might employ DEM to balance between making immediate, data-driven decisions (Directive Mode) and exploring alternative investment strategies based on emerging trends or anomalies (Exploratory Mode).

Ethical Considerations and Autonomous Decision-Making

As AI systems become more autonomous and integrated into critical aspects of society, ethical considerations will play an increasingly central role in their development and deployment.

- **Ethics of Autonomous Decision-Making (Lin, 2016):**
  - The ethics of autonomous decision-making in AI involve complex questions about accountability, transparency, and the potential for unintended consequences. As AI systems gain more autonomy, it becomes essential to establish clear ethical guidelines to govern their actions and decisions.
  - DEM can contribute to these ethical frameworks by providing a structured approach to decision-making that balances directive actions with exploratory considerations, ensuring that AI systems do not act impulsively or without adequate reflection on the potential outcomes.
- **Transparency and Explainability:**
  - As AI systems become more complex, ensuring transparency and explainability will be critical for maintaining user trust and societal acceptance. Systems that integrate DEM should be designed to clearly communicate the reasoning behind their decisions, particularly in high-stakes situations where the consequences of AI actions could have significant moral or legal implications.
  - Explainable AI (XAI) techniques will be essential for making the decision-making processes of DEM-integrated AI

systems understandable to users and stakeholders, helping to bridge the gap between human and machine reasoning.

- **Long-Term Impacts on Society**:
  - The long-term impacts of DEM in AI on society are still largely speculative but could include profound changes in how we interact with technology, make decisions, and even understand concepts like personality and identity. As AI systems become more adept at simulating human behaviors and making autonomous decisions, it will be crucial to consider the broader societal implications of these developments.
  - Ongoing research and dialogue will be necessary to navigate the ethical challenges posed by these advancements, ensuring that the benefits of AI are realized in a way that is equitable, responsible, and aligned with human values.

Conclusion

Chapter 8 has explored the speculative future applications of the Dual Mode Elicitation Model (DEM) in AI, focusing on the development of Digital Continuance Profiles, self-determining AI systems, and the integration of emerging technologies such as VR/AR, neuromemristive systems, and quantum decision theory. The potential of DEM to influence these developments is immense, offering a framework for creating AI systems that are not only more adaptive and responsive but also more aligned with human ethical standards. As AI continues to evolve, the ongoing refinement of DEM and its applications will be crucial for ensuring that these technologies contribute positively to society.

IO.

Enhancing Teaching with DEM

Introduction

The application of the Dual Mode Elicitation Model (DEM) in educational settings offers a powerful approach to balancing teaching methods and enhancing student engagement. By integrating directive and exploratory modes of communication, educators can create dynamic and interactive learning environments that cater to diverse student needs and promote deeper understanding. This chapter explores how DEM can be applied in the classroom, drawing on relevant research from constructivist learning theory, educational psychology, instructional design, social learning theory, and behavioral economics in education. Through detailed case studies and practical applications, we will demonstrate the potential of DEM to transform teaching practices and foster a more engaging and effective learning experience.

Theoretical Foundations for Applying DEM in Education

The integration of DEM into educational practices is grounded in several key theoretical frameworks that emphasize the importance of balancing structured guidance with opportunities for exploration and discovery.

- **Constructivist Learning Theory (Piaget, 1972; Vygotsky, 1978):**
    - Constructivist learning theory posits that students construct their understanding and knowledge of the world through experiences and reflecting on those experiences. This theory supports the use of DEM in education by emphasizing the need for both directive (teacher-led) and exploratory (student-led) approaches to facilitate

meaningful learning.

- ◦ In a DEM-enhanced classroom, the Directive Mode can be used to introduce new concepts and provide the necessary structure for understanding foundational knowledge. The Exploratory Mode then allows students to engage with the material more deeply through activities that encourage inquiry, experimentation, and application of concepts in new contexts.

- **Educational Psychology and Cognitive Development (Bruner, 1960; Bloom, 1956)**:

  - ◦ Educational psychology provides insights into how students learn, process information, and develop cognitively. Jerome Bruner's spiral curriculum, for example, advocates for revisiting concepts at increasing levels of complexity, which aligns with the DEM approach of gradually shifting from directive to exploratory modes as students build their understanding.

  - ◦ Bloom's taxonomy of educational objectives also supports the application of DEM by highlighting the progression from basic knowledge acquisition (Directive Mode) to higher-order thinking skills such as analysis, synthesis, and evaluation (Exploratory Mode).

- **Instructional Design Principles (Merrill, 2002; Gagné, 1985)**:

  - ◦ Instructional design principles provide a structured framework for developing effective teaching strategies that align with DEM. For instance, Gagné's Nine Events of Instruction emphasize the importance of gaining attention, presenting content, and providing feedback—elements that are well-suited to the Directive Mode.

  - ◦ At the same time, instructional design also recognizes the importance of fostering learner autonomy and encouraging exploration, which are key aspects of the Exploratory Mode. By integrating these principles with

DEM, educators can create lessons that balance direct instruction with opportunities for students to explore and apply their knowledge.

Balancing Directive and Exploratory Teaching Methods with DEM

One of the core strengths of DEM is its ability to balance directive and exploratory teaching methods, allowing educators to provide structure while also encouraging student-led inquiry and discovery.

- **Directive Mode in Teaching**:
    - The Directive Mode in teaching is characterized by clear, structured instruction that guides students through the learning process. This mode is particularly effective for introducing new concepts, providing explicit instruction on complex topics, and ensuring that all students acquire essential knowledge and skills.
    - For example, in a mathematics class, the teacher might use the Directive Mode to explain a new formula, demonstrate its application through worked examples, and ensure that students understand the steps involved in solving related problems.
- **Exploratory Mode in Teaching**:
    - The Exploratory Mode encourages students to take an active role in their learning by engaging in activities that promote inquiry, creativity, and critical thinking. This mode allows students to explore topics in greater depth, ask questions, and apply their knowledge in novel ways.
    - In the same mathematics class, after the initial directive instruction, the teacher might shift to the Exploratory Mode by giving students a complex, real-world problem that requires them to apply the formula in a new context. Students could work in groups to explore different approaches to the problem, fostering collaboration and deeper understanding.
- **Integrating Modes for Dynamic Learning**:

- Effective teaching with DEM involves seamlessly integrating directive and exploratory modes to create a dynamic learning environment. This integration allows teachers to adjust their approach based on the needs of the students, the complexity of the material, and the goals of the lesson.
- For instance, a science teacher might begin a lesson with a directive lecture on the principles of ecology, followed by an exploratory lab activity where students design and conduct experiments to observe ecological interactions in a simulated environment. The teacher can then return to the Directive Mode to guide a class discussion that synthesizes the findings and reinforces key concepts.

The Role of Social Learning Theory in DEM-Enhanced Classrooms

Albert Bandura's social learning theory emphasizes the importance of observation, imitation, and modeling in learning, which aligns closely with the principles of DEM.

- **Modeling and Observational Learning**:
    - Social learning theory suggests that students learn not only through direct instruction but also by observing and imitating the behaviors of others. In a DEM-enhanced classroom, teachers can use modeling to demonstrate both directive and exploratory approaches to problem-solving, encouraging students to adopt these strategies in their learning.
    - For example, a teacher might model how to approach a complex text analytically (Directive Mode) and then encourage students to explore different interpretations and connections (Exploratory Mode) in group discussions or individual projects.
- **Encouraging Collaborative Learning**:
    - Social learning theory also supports the use of collaborative learning activities, where students learn from

each other's experiences and perspectives. In a DEM framework, collaborative learning can be facilitated through group work that combines directive guidance with exploratory tasks.

- For instance, students might work in groups to research a historical event, with the teacher providing directive scaffolding to ensure that they understand key facts and timelines. The groups could then engage in exploratory discussions to analyze the event's causes and consequences, drawing on each member's insights and interpretations.

Behavioral Economics in Education: Enhancing Engagement with DEM

Behavioral economics, as explored by Thaler and Sunstein (2008), provides valuable insights into how to design educational environments that motivate and engage students.

- **Nudging and Choice Architecture in the Classroom:**
  - Behavioral economics introduces the concept of "nudging," where subtle changes in the environment can influence behavior in predictable ways. In the context of DEM, nudges can be used to encourage students to engage more fully with both directive and exploratory learning activities.
  - For example, a teacher might design a choice architecture that nudges students towards exploring additional resources or attempting more challenging problems by offering small incentives, such as extra credit or recognition, for completing these tasks.
- **Incentivizing Exploration and Mastery:**
  - By applying behavioral economics principles, educators can create systems that incentivize not only the completion of directive tasks but also the pursuit of exploratory learning. This approach encourages students

to take ownership of their learning and to seek out opportunities for deeper engagement with the material.

- For instance, a points-based system might reward students for participating in exploratory activities such as independent research projects, peer teaching, or creative problem-solving challenges. These incentives can help balance the focus on mastery of basic skills with the development of higher-order thinking abilities.

Case Studies and Practical Applications of DEM in Education

To illustrate the practical application of DEM in educational settings, this section presents several case studies that demonstrate how DEM can be used to enhance teaching and learning.

- **Case Study 1: Flipped Classroom Model**:
  - **Context**: A high school science teacher implements a flipped classroom model, where students are introduced to new material through instructional videos (Directive Mode) at home and then engage in exploratory, hands-on activities during class time.
  - **Application of DEM**: The teacher uses the Directive Mode to deliver content through videos, ensuring that all students have a foundational understanding before class. In the classroom, the teacher shifts to the Exploratory Mode, facilitating labs, group projects, and discussions that allow students to apply their knowledge in practical and creative ways.
  - **Outcomes**: Students show increased engagement and a deeper understanding of the material, as they are able to explore and apply concepts in a more interactive and student-centered environment.
- **Case Study 2: Project-Based Learning in Social Studies**:
  - **Context**: A social studies teacher adopts a project-based learning approach to explore the impact of global trade on local communities. The project requires students to

research, analyze, and present their findings on how trade policies affect different stakeholders.

- **Application of DEM**: The teacher uses the Directive Mode to introduce key concepts and guide students in their initial research. As the project progresses, the teacher transitions to the Exploratory Mode, encouraging students to explore various perspectives, collaborate with peers, and develop their own conclusions.
- **Outcomes**: Students develop critical thinking and problem-solving skills, as well as a deeper understanding of the complexities of global trade. The integration of directive and exploratory modes helps students navigate the research process while fostering creativity and independent thought.

- **Case Study 3: Differentiated Instruction in a Mixed-Ability Classroom:**

  - **Context**: A language arts teacher uses differentiated instruction to meet the needs of students with varying levels of ability and learning styles in a mixed-ability classroom.
  - **Application of DEM**: The teacher employs the Directive Mode to provide structured support for students who need additional guidance, using targeted mini-lessons and scaffolding techniques. For more advanced students, the teacher shifts to the Exploratory Mode, offering independent reading and writing projects that challenge them to delve deeper into literary analysis.
  - **Outcomes**: All students benefit from instruction tailored to their individual needs, with the DEM framework allowing the teacher to balance direct instruction with opportunities for self-directed learning. This approach leads to improved student outcomes across the ability spectrum, as each student is supported and challenged at their appropriate level.

Future Research Directions and Tools for Educators

The application of DEM in education offers numerous opportunities for future research and the development of new tools to support educators.

- **Research on DEM and Student Outcomes**:
  - Future research could explore the impact of DEM on student outcomes across different subjects, age groups, and educational settings. Studies could investigate how the balance of directive and exploratory teaching methods influences student engagement, retention of knowledge, and the development of critical thinking skills.
  - Longitudinal studies could also examine the long-term effects of DEM on students' academic success and personal development, providing insights into how this approach shapes learners over time.
- **Development of DEM-Based Educational Tools**:
  - There is significant potential for the development of educational tools that incorporate DEM principles. For example, adaptive learning platforms could be designed to switch between directive and exploratory modes based on student performance and engagement, providing personalized learning experiences that evolve with the learner.
  - Additionally, professional development programs for educators could be created to train teachers in the effective implementation of DEM in their classrooms, equipping them with the skills and strategies needed to balance directive and exploratory teaching methods.
- **Integration of Technology and DEM**:
  - The integration of technology with DEM offers exciting possibilities for enhancing teaching and learning. Future research could explore how digital tools, such as interactive simulations, virtual reality, and AI-powered

tutoring systems, can be used to support the dynamic integration of directive and exploratory modes in education.

- These technologies could enable more personalized and immersive learning experiences, allowing students to engage with content in ways that are tailored to their individual needs and preferences.

Conclusion

Chapter 9 has provided a comprehensive exploration of how the Dual Mode Elicitation Model (DEM) can be applied in educational settings to balance teaching methods and enhance student engagement. By integrating insights from constructivist learning theory, educational psychology, instructional design, social learning theory, and behavioral economics, this chapter has demonstrated the potential of DEM to transform teaching practices and create dynamic, interactive learning environments. The case studies presented offer practical examples of how DEM can be implemented in the classroom, while the discussion of future research directions highlights the ongoing potential for innovation in this field. As educators continue to explore and refine the use of DEM, its application in education holds great promise for improving student outcomes and fostering a deeper, more meaningful learning experience.

II.

DEM in Learning and Development

Introduction

In an increasingly complex and dynamic world, the ability to learn autonomously and think critically is essential. The Dual Mode Elicitation Model (DEM) offers a powerful framework for fostering self-directed learning and critical thinking within educational programs. By integrating insights from self-regulated learning, educational technology, critical thinking frameworks, behavioral biology, and quantum cognition, DEM can enhance the learning and development process, making it more adaptive, personalized, and effective. This chapter explores the role of DEM in learning and development, providing practical tools, case studies, and suggestions for future research in educational technology.

Self-Directed Learning and DEM

Self-directed learning (SDL) refers to the process by which learners take initiative and responsibility for their learning, setting their own goals, selecting resources, and evaluating their progress. DEM plays a crucial role in supporting SDL by balancing structured guidance with opportunities for exploration and discovery.

- **Self-Regulated Learning (Zimmerman, 2002):**
  - Self-regulated learning (SRL) is a key component of SDL, involving the active management of one's learning processes through goal-setting, self-monitoring, and self-reflection. SRL aligns closely with the principles of DEM, as it requires both directive and exploratory approaches to be effective.
  - In a DEM framework, the Directive Mode can help learners establish clear goals, plan their learning activities, and

monitor their progress. The Exploratory Mode, on the other hand, encourages learners to explore new topics, experiment with different learning strategies, and reflect on their learning experiences, fostering deeper engagement and autonomy.

- **Applying DEM to Foster SDL:**
  - DEM can be applied in educational programs to create environments that support SDL by providing a balance of structure and freedom. For instance, an online course might use the Directive Mode to deliver core content and outline learning objectives, while offering a range of exploratory activities, such as research projects, discussions, and problem-solving exercises, that allow learners to take control of their learning journey.
  - Tools such as learning management systems (LMS) can be designed to incorporate DEM principles, offering personalized learning paths that adjust based on the learner's progress and preferences, ensuring that they receive the right balance of guidance and independence.

Critical Thinking and DEM

Critical thinking is the ability to analyze, evaluate, and synthesize information to make informed decisions. It is a fundamental skill in both education and life, and DEM provides a structured approach to developing and enhancing this skill.

- **Critical Thinking Frameworks (Paul & Elder, 2006):**
  - Critical thinking frameworks, such as the Paul-Elder model, emphasize the importance of clarity, accuracy, precision, relevance, depth, breadth, logic, and fairness in thinking. These elements can be integrated into the DEM framework to guide the development of critical thinking skills.
  - The Directive Mode in DEM can be used to introduce critical thinking concepts and provide structured practice

in applying these concepts to specific problems. The Exploratory Mode allows learners to engage in open-ended discussions, debate different viewpoints, and explore complex issues from multiple perspectives, deepening their understanding and enhancing their critical thinking abilities.

- **Promoting Critical Thinking with DEM:**

  - Educators can use DEM to design activities that promote critical thinking by combining directive instruction with exploratory challenges. For example, in a history class, the teacher might begin with a lecture (Directive Mode) that outlines the key events of a historical period. Students could then engage in a debate or simulation (Exploratory Mode) where they must apply their critical thinking skills to analyze the motivations of historical figures and the consequences of their actions.

  - Digital tools, such as interactive simulations and scenario-based learning platforms, can be developed to incorporate DEM, offering learners opportunities to practice critical thinking in a variety of contexts and through different media.

Behavioral Biology and Learning Processes

Behavioral biology examines how biological factors influence behavior, including learning. Integrating insights from behavioral biology into DEM can help educators design learning environments that are aligned with the natural learning processes of the brain.

- **Behavioral Biology's Influence on Learning (Zull, 2002):**

  - The brain's natural learning processes involve cycles of observation, reflection, experimentation, and consolidation. DEM supports these processes by providing a framework for balancing the need for structured learning (Directive Mode) with the opportunity for exploration and discovery (Exploratory Mode).

- ○ For example, research has shown that the brain is more likely to retain information that is encountered in a meaningful, context-rich environment. In a DEM-enhanced classroom, educators can create such environments by using the Directive Mode to introduce core concepts and the Exploratory Mode to engage students in hands-on activities, discussions, and projects that allow them to apply and internalize what they have learned.
- **Neuroscience and Adaptive Learning**:
  - ○ Advances in neuroscience have provided deeper insights into how the brain adapts and learns. These insights can be applied to DEM by designing learning experiences that align with the brain's natural rhythms and tendencies.
  - ○ For instance, incorporating periods of rest and reflection into the learning process (Exploratory Mode) can enhance memory consolidation and problem-solving abilities, while structured review sessions (Directive Mode) can reinforce key concepts and ensure that learners retain critical information.

Quantum Cognition and Learning

Quantum cognition is an emerging field that applies principles from quantum mechanics to model cognitive processes. It offers a novel perspective on decision-making, problem-solving, and learning, which can be integrated into DEM to enhance educational programs.

- **Quantum Decision Theory (Busemeyer & Bruza, 2012)**:
  - ○ Quantum decision theory suggests that cognitive processes, such as decision-making and problem-solving, can be modeled as probabilistic events, where multiple potential outcomes are considered simultaneously. This approach aligns with the Exploratory Mode in DEM, where learners are encouraged to explore different possibilities

and consider alternative perspectives before making decisions.

- In educational programs, quantum cognition can be used to design activities that challenge learners to think probabilistically and consider the range of possible outcomes before arriving at a conclusion. This can be particularly useful in subjects such as mathematics, science, and philosophy, where uncertainty and ambiguity are often present.

- **Applying Quantum Cognition in DEM**:

  - DEM can incorporate quantum cognition principles by designing learning experiences that encourage students to embrace uncertainty and explore multiple possibilities. For example, in a science lab, students might be tasked with conducting experiments where they must consider various hypotheses and predict different outcomes (Exploratory Mode) before synthesizing their findings into a coherent explanation (Directive Mode).

  - Educational technologies, such as interactive simulations that model quantum processes, can also be used to help students understand and apply quantum cognition concepts in real-world contexts.

Case Studies and Practical Applications of DEM in Learning and Development

To illustrate the practical application of DEM in learning and development, this section presents several case studies that demonstrate how DEM can be used to foster self-directed learning, critical thinking, and adaptive learning processes.

- **Case Study 1: Online Learning Platform for Self-Directed Learning**:

  - **Context**: An online learning platform is designed to support adult learners pursuing professional development courses. The platform integrates DEM principles to balance structured learning paths with opportunities for self-directed exploration.

- ○ **Application of DEM**: The platform uses the Directive Mode to deliver course content through video lectures, readings, and quizzes, ensuring that learners acquire essential knowledge and skills. Learners are then encouraged to engage in exploratory activities, such as research projects, case studies, and peer discussions, where they can apply their learning in real-world scenarios.
- ○ **Outcomes**: Learners report higher levels of engagement and satisfaction, as they are able to tailor their learning experiences to their individual needs and interests. The balance of directive and exploratory modes also leads to improved retention of knowledge and the development of critical thinking skills.

- **Case Study 2: Critical Thinking Development in a Liberal Arts Program**:

  - ○ **Context**: A liberal arts college integrates DEM into its curriculum to enhance students' critical thinking abilities. The program emphasizes the analysis and evaluation of complex texts and ideas across various disciplines.
  - ○ **Application of DEM**: Professors use the Directive Mode to introduce key concepts, frameworks, and methodologies that students need to analyze texts critically. The Exploratory Mode is employed in seminar discussions, group projects, and writing assignments, where students are encouraged to explore different interpretations and synthesize their own arguments.
  - ○ **Outcomes**: Students demonstrate significant improvements in their ability to think critically, articulate complex ideas, and engage in meaningful dialogue. The DEM framework helps students balance the need for structured learning with the freedom to explore and challenge established ideas.

- **Case Study 3: Adaptive Learning in a STEM Program**:

- **Context**: A university STEM program incorporates DEM into its instructional design to support adaptive learning and help students master complex scientific concepts.
- **Application of DEM**: Instructors use the Directive Mode to teach foundational theories and principles through lectures and guided practice. The Exploratory Mode is integrated into lab sessions, where students design and conduct their own experiments, and in problem-based learning activities, where they work in teams to solve real-world challenges.
- **Outcomes**: Students gain a deeper understanding of STEM subjects and develop the ability to apply their knowledge in practical settings. The combination of directive instruction and exploratory learning fosters creativity, collaboration, and critical thinking, preparing students for careers in science, technology, engineering, and mathematics.

Future Research Directions and Tools for Learning and Development

The application of DEM in learning and development offers numerous opportunities for future research and the development of new tools to enhance education.

- **Research on DEM and Learning Outcomes**:
    - Future research could explore the impact of DEM on learning outcomes across different age groups, subjects, and educational contexts. Studies could examine how the balance of directive and exploratory modes influences students' ability to self-direct their learning, think critically, and adapt to new information.
    - Longitudinal studies could also investigate the long-term effects of DEM on learners' academic and career success, providing insights into how this approach shapes lifelong learning and development.

- **Development of DEM-Based Educational Technologies**:
  - There is significant potential for the development of educational technologies that incorporate DEM principles. For example, adaptive learning platforms could be designed to dynamically adjust the balance of directive and exploratory activities based on students' progress and preferences, offering personalized learning experiences that support both mastery and creativity.
  - Virtual and augmented reality tools could also be developed to provide immersive learning experiences that integrate DEM, allowing students to explore complex concepts in a hands-on, interactive environment.
- **Integration of Behavioral Biology and Quantum Cognition in Learning Design**:
  - Future research could explore how insights from behavioral biology and quantum cognition can be further integrated into DEM-based learning designs. This research could lead to the development of new instructional strategies and technologies that align with the brain's natural learning processes and encourage probabilistic thinking and decision-making.
  - Studies could also investigate how these insights can be used to design learning environments that are more adaptive, personalized, and effective in fostering deep learning and critical thinking.

Conclusion

Chapter 10 has provided a comprehensive exploration of how the Dual Mode Elicitation Model (DEM) can be applied in learning and development to foster self-directed learning, critical thinking, and adaptive learning processes. By integrating insights from self-regulated learning, educational technology, critical thinking frameworks, behavioral biology, and quantum cognition, this chapter has demonstrated the potential of DEM to transform educational programs and enhance student outcomes. The case studies presented offer practical examples of how DEM can be implemented in various educational contexts, while the discussion of future research directions highlights the ongoing potential for innovation in this field. As educators and researchers continue to explore and refine the use of DEM, its application in learning and development holds great promise for preparing learners to thrive in an increasingly complex and dynamic world.

12.

Training Educators in DEM

Introduction

The Dual Mode Elicitation Model (DEM) offers a powerful framework for enhancing teaching and learning, but its successful implementation requires that educators are properly trained to utilize its principles effectively. This chapter focuses on developing curricula and training programs that equip educators with the skills necessary to apply DEM in their teaching practices. Drawing on research in teacher training methodologies, curriculum development, educational psychology, neuroscience of learning, and phenomenological control, this chapter provides comprehensive guidelines for educator training. Additionally, case studies, methodologies, and future research suggestions are included to support the development of robust teacher education programs grounded in DEM principles.

Foundations of Teacher Training in DEM

Teacher training is a critical component of successful educational outcomes. Training educators in DEM requires a deep understanding of both the model's principles and the pedagogical strategies that align with those principles.

- **Teacher Training Methodologies (Darling-Hammond, 2006):**
  - Effective teacher training programs incorporate a combination of theoretical knowledge and practical experience. For DEM, this means providing educators with a solid understanding of the model's theoretical foundations, as well as opportunities to practice applying DEM principles in real-world teaching scenarios.
  - Training programs should include workshops, seminars,

and hands-on activities that allow educators to explore the Directive and Exploratory Modes of DEM, understand when and how to apply each mode, and reflect on their experiences through peer feedback and self-assessment.

- **Curriculum Development for Teacher Training (Posner & Rudnitsky, 2006)**:
  - Developing a curriculum for training educators in DEM involves designing content that is both comprehensive and adaptable to different educational contexts. The curriculum should cover the core principles of DEM, including its theoretical underpinnings, practical applications, and strategies for integrating DEM into various teaching practices.
  - The curriculum should also be flexible enough to accommodate the diverse needs of educators, from those working in early childhood education to those in higher education or specialized training programs. This flexibility ensures that all educators can find relevance and applicability in DEM, regardless of their teaching context.

Neuroscience of Learning and Teacher Training

Understanding the neuroscience of learning is essential for educators who wish to apply DEM effectively. Insights from neuroscience can inform the design of teacher training programs, helping educators understand how students learn and how to create environments that support optimal learning.

- **Neuroscience of Learning (Zull, 2002)**:
  - The neuroscience of learning focuses on how the brain processes, stores, and retrieves information. Key concepts include neural plasticity, which refers to the brain's ability to change and adapt in response to new experiences, and reinforcement, which is the process by which behaviors are strengthened or weakened based on outcomes.
  - In the context of DEM, educators need to understand how

directive and exploratory teaching methods engage different neural processes. For example, the Directive Mode may activate areas of the brain associated with structured, linear thinking, while the Exploratory Mode may engage regions involved in creativity and problem-solving. Teacher training programs should incorporate this knowledge, helping educators design lessons that align with the brain's natural learning processes.

- **Plasticity and Reinforcement in Teaching Practices**:

  - Teacher training programs should emphasize the importance of plasticity and reinforcement in shaping student learning. Educators can use DEM to create learning experiences that encourage neural growth and adaptability by alternating between directive instruction and exploratory activities.
  - For instance, after teaching a new concept using the Directive Mode, educators might design reinforcement activities that allow students to explore and apply the concept in novel ways, thereby strengthening their understanding and promoting long-term retention.

Phenomenological Control in Learning

Phenomenological control refers to the ability to influence one's subjective experiences, and it plays a significant role in both teaching and learning. Integrating insights from phenomenological control into teacher training can enhance educators' ability to model and teach complex concepts effectively.

- **Phenomenological Control in Education (Carhart-Harris & Friston, 2010)**:

  - In educational contexts, phenomenological control can be understood as the ability of educators to guide students' attention, perceptions, and interpretations during the learning process. This involves helping students to focus on relevant information, make meaningful connections between concepts, and develop a coherent understanding of the material.

  - Teacher training programs should include strategies for applying phenomenological control in the classroom. For example, educators might learn techniques for directing students' attention during lectures (Directive Mode) or facilitating open-ended discussions that encourage students to explore different perspectives (Exploratory Mode).

- **Modeling Complex Concepts through DEM:**

  - DEM can be used to model complex concepts by guiding students through a structured learning process that gradually shifts from directive to exploratory modes. Teacher training programs should equip educators with the skills to design lessons that scaffold student learning, starting with clear explanations and gradually encouraging independent exploration and discovery.

  - For instance, in a science class, educators might begin with a directive lesson on the principles of genetics, followed by an exploratory activity where students simulate genetic crosses and predict outcomes. By modeling the process of scientific inquiry, educators can help students develop a deeper understanding of complex concepts.

Developing and Implementing DEM-Based Training Programs

To ensure that educators are well-prepared to implement DEM in their classrooms, training programs must be carefully developed and effectively implemented.

- **Designing DEM-Based Training Programs:**

  - Training programs should be designed with a clear understanding of the goals and outcomes associated with DEM. This includes identifying the specific skills and knowledge educators need to effectively apply DEM in their teaching practices, as well as the methods for assessing their progress.

- A DEM-based training program might include modules on the theoretical foundations of DEM, practical applications in various educational contexts, and strategies for integrating DEM into curriculum design and instructional practices. Each module should include both instructional content and opportunities for hands-on practice, reflection, and feedback.

- **Implementing Training Programs in Educational Settings**:

  - Implementation of DEM-based training programs should be flexible and responsive to the needs of educators. This may involve offering training in various formats, such as in-person workshops, online courses, or blended learning experiences, to accommodate different learning preferences and schedules.

  - Ongoing support is also crucial for successful implementation. This could include mentoring programs, peer collaboration opportunities, and access to resources that help educators refine their DEM practices over time.

- **Case Studies of DEM-Based Training Programs**:

  - **Case Study 1: DEM Training for K-12 Educators**:

    - **Context**: A school district implements a DEM-based training program for K-12 educators, focusing on integrating directive and exploratory teaching methods across all grade levels.

    - **Implementation**: The program includes a series of workshops that cover the principles of DEM, practical applications in different subject areas, and strategies for adapting DEM to meet the needs of diverse learners. Educators participate in hands-on activities, collaborative lesson planning, and peer feedback sessions.

    - **Outcomes**: Educators report increased confidence in

their ability to balance directive and exploratory teaching methods, leading to more dynamic and engaging classroom environments. Student engagement and achievement improve as teachers become more adept at using DEM to support learning.

- ○ **Case Study 2: DEM in Higher Education Faculty Development:**

  - **Context**: A university launches a faculty development program to train professors in using DEM to enhance their teaching practices in undergraduate and graduate courses.
  - **Implementation**: The program includes seminars on the neuroscience of learning, phenomenological control, and the application of DEM in higher education. Faculty members work in interdisciplinary teams to develop and implement DEM-based curricula, with ongoing support from instructional designers and educational technologists.
  - **Outcomes**: Faculty members successfully integrate DEM into their courses, resulting in improved student engagement, critical thinking, and academic performance. The interdisciplinary collaboration fosters innovation in curriculum design and teaching practices.

Future Research Directions in Teacher Education and DEM

As the application of DEM in education continues to evolve, there are numerous opportunities for future research in teacher education.

- **Research on the Impact of DEM on Teacher Effectiveness**:

  - ○ Future research could explore the impact of DEM-based training on teacher effectiveness, including how well educators are able to implement DEM principles in their classrooms and the resulting effects on student outcomes.

Studies could investigate the relationship between teacher training in DEM and improvements in student engagement, achievement, and critical thinking skills.

- Longitudinal studies could also examine the long-term effects of DEM training on teachers' professional development and career satisfaction, providing insights into the sustainability and scalability of DEM-based teacher education programs.

- **Development of DEM-Specific Pedagogical Tools**:

  - There is significant potential for the development of pedagogical tools specifically designed to support the application of DEM in teacher education. These tools might include digital platforms that offer personalized training experiences, virtual simulations that allow educators to practice applying DEM in different classroom scenarios, and assessment tools that measure the effectiveness of DEM implementation.

  - Research could also focus on the development of instructional materials, such as lesson plans, activity guides, and assessment rubrics, that align with DEM principles and support educators in creating DEM-based learning environments.

- **Exploration of Cross-Cultural Applications of DEM in Teacher Training**:

  - As DEM is applied in diverse educational contexts around the world, it is important to explore how

its principles can be adapted to meet the needs of different cultural and educational settings. Future research could investigate how DEM-based teacher training programs can be tailored to respect and incorporate local teaching practices, cultural values, and educational goals.

- **Cross-Cultural Applications in Practice**:

- Researchers could study the implementation of DEM in various cultural contexts, examining how the balance of directive and exploratory teaching methods is perceived and applied in different educational systems. For example, in collectivist cultures where collaborative learning is emphasized, the Exploratory Mode might be more naturally integrated, while the Directive Mode may require adaptation to align with cultural expectations of authority and instruction.
- Comparative studies could also be conducted to identify best practices for adapting DEM to different cultural contexts, providing insights into how global educational initiatives can benefit from the model while respecting local traditions and pedagogies.

Conclusion

Chapter 11 has provided a comprehensive exploration of training educators in the Dual Mode Elicitation Model (DEM), offering guidelines for developing and implementing curricula and training programs that equip educators with the skills to use DEM effectively. By integrating insights from teacher training methodologies, curriculum development, educational psychology, neuroscience of learning, and phenomenological control, this chapter has demonstrated how DEM can enhance teaching practices and improve student outcomes. The case studies presented offer practical examples of how DEM-based training programs can be implemented in various educational settings, while the discussion of future research directions highlights the ongoing potential for innovation in teacher education. As educators continue to refine their use of DEM, the model's application in teacher training holds great promise for preparing teachers to meet the challenges of modern education and to support the development of engaged, autonomous learners.

13.

DEM in Therapeutic Settings

Introduction

The Dual Mode Elicitation Model (DEM) offers a dynamic framework for enhancing therapeutic practices by improving communication between therapists and patients. By integrating directive and exploratory modes of communication, DEM can be applied in various therapeutic settings to optimize patient outcomes. This chapter explores the application of DEM in therapy, focusing on how it can enhance communication, strengthen the therapeutic relationship, and improve overall therapeutic outcomes. Drawing on relevant research from cognitive-behavioral therapy (CBT), psychodynamic theory, patient-centered care, neuroscience, behavioral psychology, and phenomenological control, this chapter provides a comprehensive guide to using DEM in therapeutic contexts. Case studies illustrate the practical application of DEM, and future research directions are suggested to further refine and expand its use in therapy.

Theoretical Foundations of DEM in Therapy

The integration of DEM into therapeutic practices is supported by several foundational theories in psychology and therapy, each contributing to the understanding of how directive and exploratory communication can enhance therapeutic outcomes.

- **Cognitive-Behavioral Therapy (CBT) (Beck, 2011):**
  - CBT is a widely used therapeutic approach that focuses on identifying and modifying dysfunctional thought patterns and behaviors. The Directive Mode in DEM aligns closely with the structured, goal-oriented techniques used in CBT, such as cognitive restructuring and behavioral activation.

By providing clear, directive guidance, therapists can help patients develop practical strategies for managing their symptoms and improving their mental health.

- The Exploratory Mode in DEM complements CBT by encouraging patients to explore the underlying causes of their thoughts and behaviors, fostering a deeper understanding of their emotional and cognitive processes. This mode can be particularly useful in helping patients identify and challenge cognitive distortions or explore alternative perspectives.

- **Psychodynamic Theory (Freud, 1917; Jung, 1961):**

  - Psychodynamic theory emphasizes the exploration of unconscious processes, childhood experiences, and the internal conflicts that influence behavior. The Exploratory Mode in DEM is particularly well-suited to psychodynamic therapy, as it encourages open-ended dialogue, free association, and the exploration of unconscious material.

  - The Directive Mode can be used in psychodynamic therapy to guide patients through structured exercises, such as dream analysis or the interpretation of transference, helping them gain insight into their unconscious motivations and relational patterns.

- **Patient-Centered Care (Rogers, 1951):**

  - Patient-centered care is an approach that prioritizes the patient's needs, preferences, and values in the therapeutic process. DEM supports patient-centered care by providing a flexible framework that can be tailored to the individual needs of each patient. The Directive Mode ensures that the patient's immediate concerns are addressed with clear and actionable guidance, while the Exploratory Mode allows the patient to engage in self-exploration and expression.

  - By balancing directive and exploratory communication, therapists can create a therapeutic environment that is both supportive and empowering, helping patients feel understood and respected.

Neuroscience of Therapeutic Relationships

Understanding the neuroscience behind therapeutic relationships can provide valuable insights into how DEM can be applied to enhance these relationships and improve patient outcomes.

- **Mirror Neurons and Empathy (Gallese, 2003):**
    - Mirror neurons are a type of neuron that fires both when an individual performs an action and when they observe someone else performing the same action. These neurons are thought to play a crucial role in empathy and the development of therapeutic rapport. By mirroring the patient's emotions and behaviors, therapists can create a sense of attunement and understanding, which is critical for building trust and facilitating therapeutic change.
    - The Exploratory Mode in DEM can be particularly effective in activating mirror neurons, as it encourages the therapist to engage in reflective listening, empathy, and validation of the patient's experiences. This mode allows the therapist to connect with the patient on a deeper emotional level, fostering a stronger therapeutic alliance.
- **Neuroplasticity and Behavioral Change (Kandel, 2006):**
    - Neuroplasticity refers to the brain's ability to reorganize itself by forming new neural connections throughout life. This concept is central to understanding how therapy can lead to lasting behavioral change. The Directive Mode in DEM can be used to reinforce positive behaviors and cognitive patterns, helping patients rewire their brains in ways that support healthier functioning.
    - The Exploratory Mode allows patients to experiment with new ways of thinking and behaving, promoting neuroplasticity by encouraging the brain to adapt to new

experiences. By alternating between directive guidance and exploratory self-discovery, therapists can help patients develop more adaptive neural pathways.

Behavioral Psychology and DEM in Therapy

Behavioral psychology, with its focus on the relationship between behavior and the environment, offers valuable insights for applying DEM in therapy.

- **Skinner's Operant Conditioning (Skinner, 1953):**
  - Operant conditioning involves reinforcing desired behaviors and reducing undesired behaviors through the use of rewards and consequences. The Directive Mode in DEM aligns with this approach by providing clear instructions and feedback that help patients understand the consequences of their actions and reinforce positive behavioral changes.
  - The Exploratory Mode can be used to help patients explore the environmental factors that influence their behavior, such as triggers for maladaptive behaviors or potential reinforcers for desired behaviors. This exploration can lead to a deeper understanding of the patient's behavioral patterns and more effective strategies for change.
- **Bandura's Social Learning Theory (Bandura, 1977):**
  - Social learning theory emphasizes the role of observation, imitation, and modeling in learning new behaviors. In therapy, the Directive Mode can be used to model healthy behaviors and coping strategies, while the Exploratory Mode encourages patients to experiment with these behaviors in different contexts and reflect on their experiences.
  - By integrating DEM with social learning theory, therapists can help patients develop new skills and behaviors through a combination of guided instruction and self-directed

exploration.

Phenomenological Control in Therapy

Phenomenological control, the ability to influence one's subjective experience, is a powerful tool in therapy that can be enhanced through the application of DEM.

- **Phenomenological Control and Therapeutic Interventions (Carhart-Harris, 2014):**
  - Phenomenological control involves guiding patients to focus their attention, alter their perceptions, and engage in mental exercises that shape their subjective experiences. The Directive Mode in DEM can be used to teach patients specific techniques for exerting phenomenological control, such as mindfulness, visualization, or cognitive restructuring.
  - The Exploratory Mode allows patients to explore the effects of these techniques on their thoughts, emotions, and behaviors, fostering a deeper understanding of how they can influence their own experiences. This mode also provides space for patients to reflect on their experiences and integrate new insights into their overall therapeutic progress.
- **Enhancing Therapeutic Outcomes through Phenomenological Control:**
  - By incorporating phenomenological control into DEM-based therapy, therapists can help patients develop greater self-awareness and self-regulation. This can lead to more effective management of symptoms, improved emotional resilience, and a stronger sense of agency in the therapeutic process.
  - Case studies have shown that patients who learn to exert phenomenological control through DEM-based interventions often experience significant improvements in their mental health and well-being, as they are better

equipped to manage their thoughts and emotions in daily life.

Case Studies: DEM in Therapeutic Practice

To illustrate the practical application of DEM in therapy, this section presents several case studies from different therapeutic contexts.

- **Case Study 1: Cognitive-Behavioral Therapy for Anxiety**:
  - **Context**: A therapist uses DEM to treat a patient with generalized anxiety disorder (GAD). The patient struggles with constant worry and difficulty managing stress.
  - **Application of DEM**: The therapist uses the Directive Mode to teach the patient cognitive-behavioral techniques, such as identifying and challenging irrational thoughts and practicing relaxation exercises. In subsequent sessions, the therapist shifts to the Exploratory Mode, encouraging the patient to explore the underlying causes of their anxiety and experiment with new coping strategies in different situations.
  - **Outcomes**: The patient experiences a significant reduction in anxiety symptoms and reports feeling more in control of their thoughts and emotions. The combination of directive guidance and exploratory self-reflection helps the patient develop a more resilient and adaptive mindset.
- **Case Study 2: Psychodynamic Therapy for Depression**:
  - **Context**: A therapist applies DEM in psychodynamic therapy with a patient who is struggling with chronic depression and unresolved childhood trauma.
  - **Application of DEM**: The therapist begins with the Directive Mode, guiding the patient through structured exercises such as journaling and dream analysis to explore unconscious material. As the therapy progresses, the therapist increasingly adopts the Exploratory Mode,

facilitating open-ended discussions that allow the patient to process and integrate their emotions and experiences.

  - **Outcomes**: The patient gains greater insight into the root causes of their depression and begins to heal from past traumas. The dynamic integration of directive and exploratory communication helps the patient achieve a deeper understanding of themselves and their emotional world.

- **Case Study 3: Integrative Therapy for PTSD**:

  - **Context**: A therapist uses DEM in an integrative therapy approach to treat a patient with post-traumatic stress disorder (PTSD) resulting from a traumatic accident.

  - **Application of DEM**: The therapist employs the Directive Mode to teach the patient grounding techniques and cognitive-behavioral strategies to manage flashbacks and anxiety. The Exploratory Mode is used to help the patient process the trauma in a safe and supportive environment, exploring their emotions and memories related to the event.

  - **Outcomes**: The patient experiences a reduction in PTSD symptoms and begins to regain a sense of safety and control. The use of DEM allows the therapist to provide both the structure and flexibility needed to support the patient's recovery.

Future Research Directions in DEM-Based Therapy

As the application of DEM in therapeutic settings continues to evolve, there are numerous opportunities for future research to further refine and expand its use.

- **Research on the Efficacy of DEM in Different Therapeutic Modalities**:

  - Future research could investigate the efficacy of DEM in various therapeutic modalities, including CBT, psychodynamic therapy, and integrative approaches. Studies could explore how the balance of directive and exploratory communication influences therapeutic outcomes across different patient populations and mental health conditions.

  ○ Comparative studies could also examine the effectiveness of DEM-based therapy compared to traditional therapeutic approaches, providing insights into the unique benefits and challenges of using DEM in clinical practice.

- **Development of DEM-Based Therapeutic Tools**:

  ○ There is potential for the development of therapeutic tools and resources that incorporate DEM principles. These tools might include workbooks, guided exercises, and digital platforms that help therapists apply DEM in their practice. Research could focus on the development and validation of these tools, ensuring that they are effective and accessible to a wide range of therapists and patients.

  ○ Additionally, virtual reality (VR) and artificial intelligence (AI) could be explored as innovative ways to integrate DEM into therapeutic settings, offering immersive and personalized therapeutic experiences.

- **Exploration of Cross-Cultural Applications of DEM in Therapy**:

  ○ As DEM is applied in diverse cultural contexts, it is important to explore how its principles can be adapted to meet the needs of different populations. Future research could investigate how DEM-based therapy can be tailored to respect and incorporate cultural values, beliefs, and practices, ensuring that it is both effective and culturally sensitive.

Conclusion

Chapter 12 has provided a comprehensive exploration of how the Dual Mode Elicitation Model (DEM) can be applied in therapeutic settings to enhance patient communication and improve therapeutic outcomes. By integrating insights from cognitive-behavioral therapy, psychodynamic theory, patient-centered care, neuroscience, behavioral psychology, and phenomenological control, this chapter has demonstrated the potential of DEM to transform therapeutic practices. The case studies presented offer practical examples of how DEM can be implemented in different therapeutic contexts, while the discussion of future research directions highlights the ongoing potential for innovation in this field. As therapists continue to refine their use of DEM, its application in therapy holds great promise for improving mental health outcomes and enhancing the overall therapeutic experience.

14.

Using DEM in Patient-Centered Care

Introduction

Patient-centered care has emerged as a fundamental approach in modern healthcare, emphasizing the importance of understanding and addressing patients' needs, preferences, and values. The Dual Mode Elicitation Model (DEM) offers a powerful framework for enhancing patient-centered care by optimizing communication strategies that foster engagement, empathy, and collaboration between healthcare providers and patients. This chapter explores how DEM can be applied to improve patient-centered care, integrating insights from patient-centered care models, communication in healthcare, empathy research, evolutionary psychology, and behavioral economics. Through case studies and practical tools, this chapter demonstrates the impact of DEM on patient outcomes and offers methodologies for implementing DEM in healthcare settings.

Foundations of Patient-Centered Care and DEM

Patient-centered care is a healthcare approach that prioritizes the patient's experience and involves them as active participants in their care. The principles of DEM align closely with the core tenets of patient-centered care, offering a structured yet flexible approach to enhancing communication and engagement.

- **Patient-Centered Care Models (Epstein & Street, 2011):**

  - Patient-centered care models emphasize the importance of respect for patients' values, preferences, and needs, as well as the coordination and integration of care. These models advocate for communication strategies that are responsive to the individual patient, fostering a partnership between the patient and healthcare provider.

- ◦ DEM supports patient-centered care by offering a framework that balances directive communication, where the provider delivers clear and concise information, with exploratory communication, where the patient is encouraged to share their concerns, ask questions, and participate in decision-making. This balance ensures that care is both efficient and empathetic, addressing the patient's needs while promoting a sense of empowerment and collaboration.

- **Communication in Healthcare (Street et al., 2009)**:

  - ◦ Effective communication is a cornerstone of patient-centered care, influencing patient satisfaction, adherence to treatment, and overall health outcomes. DEM enhances communication in healthcare by providing a model that allows healthcare providers to tailor their communication style to the needs of the patient, switching between directive and exploratory modes as appropriate.

  - ◦ For example, a provider might use the Directive Mode to explain a treatment plan clearly and concisely, ensuring that the patient understands the necessary steps. The Exploratory Mode can then be used to engage the patient in a discussion about their concerns, preferences, and any barriers they may face in adhering to the treatment plan.

Empathy in Clinical Practice and DEM

Empathy is a critical component of effective patient-centered care, allowing healthcare providers to understand and respond to patients' emotions and experiences. DEM facilitates the integration of empathy into clinical practice by providing a framework for balancing structured guidance with compassionate, patient-centered communication.

- **Empathy in Clinical Practice (Decety & Fotopoulou, 2015)**:

  - ◦ Empathy in healthcare involves the ability to recognize

and understand a patient's emotional state, communicate this understanding, and respond in a way that supports the patient's well-being. Research has shown that empathy is associated with improved patient satisfaction, adherence to treatment, and overall health outcomes.

  - DEM enhances empathetic communication by incorporating both directive and exploratory modes. The Directive Mode allows providers to offer clear, supportive guidance, while the Exploratory Mode encourages open-ended conversations where patients can express their feelings and concerns. This dynamic integration ensures that patients feel heard, valued, and supported throughout their care.

- **Applying DEM to Foster Empathy**:

  - Healthcare providers can use DEM to foster empathy by starting with directive communication to establish trust and provide necessary information, then transitioning to exploratory communication to engage with the patient's emotional and psychological needs. This approach helps to build a strong therapeutic relationship, where the patient feels understood and involved in their care.

  - For instance, during a difficult diagnosis, a physician might first use the Directive Mode to explain the medical facts clearly and compassionately. They can then switch to the Exploratory Mode to explore the patient's emotional response, offer support, and discuss potential coping strategies.

Evolutionary Psychology Perspectives on Caregiving

Understanding the evolutionary basis of caregiving behaviors can provide valuable insights into how healthcare providers can enhance patient-centered care through DEM.

- **Evolutionary Psychology and Caregiving (Hrdy, 2009)**:

  - Evolutionary psychology suggests that caregiving

behaviors have evolved as adaptive strategies to ensure the survival and well-being of offspring and kin. These behaviors are characterized by empathy, nurturing, and the ability to respond to the needs of others, traits that are essential in healthcare settings.

   - DEM aligns with these caregiving behaviors by facilitating a communication style that is both nurturing and responsive. The Directive Mode reflects the structured guidance that is necessary for effective caregiving, while the Exploratory Mode allows healthcare providers to respond flexibly to the individual needs and emotions of their patients.

- **Integrating Evolutionary Perspectives with DEM:**

   - Healthcare providers can integrate evolutionary psychology with DEM by recognizing the innate caregiving instincts that drive their interactions with patients. By consciously applying DEM principles, providers can enhance these instincts with structured communication strategies that promote patient engagement and well-being.

   - For example, a nurse providing care to a patient recovering from surgery might use the Directive Mode to ensure that the patient follows post-operative instructions. At the same time, the nurse can use the Exploratory Mode to address the patient's emotional needs, offering reassurance and support as the patient navigates their recovery.

Behavioral Economics in Healthcare and DEM

Behavioral economics provides insights into how healthcare providers can influence patient behavior through communication strategies that align with DEM principles.

- **Behavioral Economics in Healthcare (Thaler & Sunstein, 2008):**

- Behavioral economics explores how psychological, social, and emotional factors influence decision-making. In healthcare, these insights can be used to design communication strategies that "nudge" patients toward healthier behaviors without restricting their autonomy.
- DEM supports the application of behavioral economics in healthcare by offering a framework for balancing directive and exploratory communication. The Directive Mode can be used to provide clear, actionable recommendations that guide patients toward desired health outcomes, while the Exploratory Mode allows for patient autonomy and engagement in decision-making.

- **Using DEM to Enhance Patient Engagement**:

  - Healthcare providers can use DEM to enhance patient engagement by combining directive communication that guides patients toward specific actions with exploratory communication that empowers them to take an active role in their care. This approach can lead to better adherence to treatment plans and improved health outcomes.
  - For instance, a healthcare provider might use the Directive Mode to recommend a specific exercise regimen for a patient with diabetes, explaining the benefits and how to get started. The provider can then switch to the Exploratory Mode to discuss the patient's preferences, potential barriers, and ways to incorporate the regimen into their daily routine, increasing the likelihood of adherence.

Case Studies: DEM in Patient-Centered Care

To illustrate the practical application of DEM in patient-centered care, this section presents several case studies from different healthcare settings.

- **Case Study 1: Enhancing Communication in Oncology Care**:

  - **Context**: An oncologist uses DEM to improve

communication with patients undergoing cancer treatment. The goal is to enhance patient understanding of complex treatment plans and support them emotionally throughout their care.

- **Application of DEM**: The oncologist uses the Directive Mode to explain treatment options, potential side effects, and the steps involved in the care plan. During follow-up visits, the oncologist shifts to the Exploratory Mode, encouraging patients to express their concerns, ask questions, and discuss how they are coping with treatment.
- **Outcomes**: Patients report higher levels of satisfaction with their care, better understanding of their treatment plans, and increased emotional support. The use of DEM helps to build strong, trust-based relationships between the oncologist and patients, leading to improved adherence to treatment and better overall outcomes.

- **Case Study 2: Patient-Centered Care in Primary Care Settings**:

  - **Context**: A primary care physician integrates DEM into routine patient visits to enhance patient engagement and improve health outcomes for chronic disease management.
  - **Application of DEM**: During initial consultations, the physician uses the Directive Mode to provide patients with clear information about their diagnosis and treatment options. The Exploratory Mode is used to involve patients in setting health goals, discussing lifestyle changes, and identifying potential challenges to managing their condition.
  - **Outcomes**: Patients become more engaged in managing their health, leading to better adherence to treatment plans and improved control of chronic conditions such as hypertension and diabetes. The combination of directive and exploratory communication fosters a collaborative

approach to care, empowering patients to take an active role in their health.

- **Case Study 3: Integrating DEM in Mental Health Services**:
    - ◦ **Context**: A mental health clinic adopts DEM to improve communication between therapists and patients, particularly in the treatment of anxiety and depression.
    - ◦ **Application of DEM**: Therapists use the Directive Mode to teach patients coping strategies and cognitive-behavioral techniques. The Exploratory Mode is employed to explore patients' thoughts, feelings, and experiences, allowing for a deeper understanding of their mental health issues and the development of personalized treatment plans.
    - ◦ **Outcomes**: Patients experience significant improvements in their mental health, reporting greater satisfaction with their therapy and a stronger therapeutic alliance. The use of DEM enables therapists to balance structured interventions with empathetic, patient-centered communication, leading to more effective treatment outcomes.

Practical Tools and Methodologies for Implementing DEM in Patient Care

To effectively implement DEM in patient-centered care, healthcare providers need practical tools and methodologies that support its integration into clinical practice.

- **Developing DEM-Based Communication Guidelines**:
    - ◦ Healthcare organizations can develop communication guidelines that incorporate DEM principles, providing healthcare providers with clear strategies for balancing directive and exploratory communication. These guidelines should include examples of how to apply DEM in different clinical scenarios, as well as tips for adjusting communication styles based on patient needs and preferences.

- Training programs can be designed to help healthcare providers develop the skills necessary to implement DEM, including workshops, role-playing exercises, and feedback sessions that focus on the practical application of DEM in patient care.

- **Using Technology to Support DEM in Healthcare**:

  - Digital tools and platforms can be developed to support the use of DEM in healthcare settings. For example, electronic health records (EHRs) could be designed to prompt healthcare providers to switch between directive and exploratory modes during patient interactions, ensuring that both types of communication are used effectively.
  - Telemedicine platforms could also integrate DEM principles, offering features that guide providers in balancing structured information delivery with patient-centered exploration during virtual visits.

- **Creating a Culture of Patient-Centered Care with DEM**:

  - Healthcare organizations can promote a culture of patient-centered care by encouraging the use of DEM across all levels of care delivery. This might involve incorporating DEM into organizational policies, training programs, and performance evaluations, as well as recognizing and rewarding providers who demonstrate excellence in patient-centered communication.
  - Ongoing support and resources should be provided to help healthcare providers refine their use of DEM, including access to mentorship, continuing education opportunities, and peer support networks.

Future Research Directions in DEM and Patient-Centered Care

As the application of DEM in patient-centered care continues to evolve, there are numerous opportunities for future research to further explore its impact and potential.

- **Research on the Impact of DEM on Patient Outcomes**:
  - ◦ Future research could investigate the impact of DEM on patient outcomes across different healthcare settings and patient populations. Studies could explore how the balance of directive and exploratory communication influences patient satisfaction, adherence to treatment, and overall health outcomes.
  - ◦ Longitudinal studies could also examine the long-term effects of DEM on patient engagement and health behaviors, providing insights into the sustainability and effectiveness of DEM-based care.
- **Development of DEM-Based Tools for Healthcare Providers**:
  - ◦ There is potential for the development of tools and resources that support the use of DEM in patient-centered care. These might include digital platforms, communication training modules, and assessment tools that help healthcare providers implement DEM in their practice.
  - ◦ Research could focus on the development and validation of these tools, ensuring that they are effective in improving patient-provider communication and enhancing patient outcomes.
- **Exploration of Cross-Cultural Applications of DEM in Healthcare**:
  - ◦ As DEM is applied in diverse healthcare settings, it is important to explore how its principles can be adapted to meet the needs of different cultural and patient populations. Future research could investigate how DEM-based care can be tailored to respect and incorporate cultural values, beliefs, and practices, ensuring that it is both effective and culturally sensitive.

Conclusion

Chapter 13 has provided a comprehensive exploration of how

the Dual Mode Elicitation Model (DEM) can be applied to enhance patient-centered care in healthcare settings. By integrating insights from patient-centered care models, communication in healthcare, empathy research, evolutionary psychology, and behavioral economics, this chapter has demonstrated the potential of DEM to transform patient care and improve health outcomes. The case studies presented offer practical examples of how DEM can be implemented in different healthcare contexts, while the discussion of practical tools and future research directions highlights the ongoing potential for innovation in this field. As healthcare providers continue to refine their use of DEM, its application in patient-centered care holds great promise for improving patient satisfaction, engagement, and overall health outcomes.

15.

Strategic Communication with DEM

Introduction

Strategic communication plays a critical role in shaping public perception, influencing behavior, and achieving organizational objectives. The Dual-Mode Elicitation Model (DEM) offers a powerful framework for crafting effective messages and engaging diverse audiences through the strategic use of directive and exploratory communication modes. This chapter explores the application of DEM in strategic communication, integrating insights from communication theory, strategic communication frameworks, public relations models, Edward Bernays' principles of propaganda, game theory, and behavioral economics. Through case studies and practical strategies, this chapter demonstrates how DEM can be used to shape public opinion and influence behavior effectively.

Foundations of Strategic Communication and DEM

Strategic communication involves the purposeful use of communication by an organization to fulfill its mission. It encompasses a wide range of activities, including public relations, marketing, and crisis communication. DEM provides a versatile framework that enhances strategic communication by allowing communicators to balance structured messaging with adaptive, audience-focused engagement.

- **Communication Theory (McLuhan, 1964; Bernays, 1928):**
  - Marshall McLuhan's famous assertion that "the medium is the message" emphasizes the importance of understanding the channels through which messages are delivered. DEM supports this principle by providing a flexible framework that can be adapted to different media,

ensuring that messages are effectively tailored to the context in which they are received.

- Edward Bernays, often considered the father of public relations, introduced the concept of propaganda as a means of shaping public opinion through strategic communication. DEM builds on Bernays' ideas by offering a structured approach to message crafting that balances persuasive intent (Directive Mode) with the need for audience engagement and feedback (Exploratory Mode).

- **Strategic Communication Frameworks (Hallahan et al., 2007):**

  - Strategic communication frameworks provide a systematic approach to designing and implementing communication strategies that align with organizational goals. These frameworks typically involve setting clear objectives, identifying target audiences, crafting messages, selecting communication channels, and evaluating outcomes.

  - DEM enhances strategic communication frameworks by integrating the flexibility to switch between directive and exploratory communication modes. This allows communicators to adapt their strategies based on real-time feedback, ensuring that messages resonate with audiences and achieve the desired impact.

Crafting Effective Messages with DEM

Effective messaging is at the heart of strategic communication. DEM offers a structured approach to crafting messages that are clear, persuasive, and adaptable to different audience needs and contexts.

- **Directive Mode in Message Crafting:**

  - The Directive Mode in DEM is used to deliver clear, concise, and authoritative messages. This mode is particularly effective in situations where the communicator needs to provide specific instructions, convey critical information, or establish a strong, persuasive argument.

- ◦ For example, in a public health campaign, the Directive Mode might be used to communicate the importance of vaccination, providing clear facts, benefits, and steps for obtaining the vaccine. This mode ensures that the audience receives unambiguous information that supports the campaign's objectives.

- **Exploratory Mode in Message Crafting**:

  - ◦ The Exploratory Mode encourages open-ended communication, inviting the audience to engage with the message, ask questions, and explore different perspectives. This mode is particularly useful in situations where the communicator seeks to foster dialogue, build relationships, or encourage the audience to consider new ideas.

  - ◦ In the context of a corporate social responsibility (CSR) initiative, the Exploratory Mode might be used to engage stakeholders in a discussion about sustainability practices, inviting them to share their views, offer feedback, and participate in shaping the company's CSR strategy.

- **Integrating Modes for Dynamic Messaging**:

  - ◦ Effective strategic communication often requires the integration of both directive and exploratory modes. Communicators can start with a directive message to establish the key points, then shift to an exploratory approach to engage the audience in a dialogue, address concerns, and adapt the message based on audience feedback.

  - ◦ For example, a political campaign might begin with a directive message outlining the candidate's key policies, followed by town hall meetings (exploratory mode) where voters can ask questions, express their concerns, and interact directly with the candidate.

Influencing Public Perception with DEM

Public perception is a powerful force that can determine the success or failure of strategic communication efforts. DEM offers a framework for shaping public perception by combining persuasive messaging with audience engagement.

- **Edward Bernays' Principles of Propaganda (Bernays, 1928):**
    - Edward Bernays' work on propaganda highlights the importance of understanding public opinion and using strategic communication to influence it. DEM supports Bernays' principles by providing a model that allows communicators to craft persuasive messages while also engaging with the audience to understand and shape their perceptions.
    - For instance, a company facing a public relations crisis might use the Directive Mode to clearly state its position and actions being taken, while employing the Exploratory Mode to engage with the public, listen to concerns, and demonstrate a commitment to transparency and accountability.
- **Game Theory in Communication Strategy (Nash, 1950):**
    - Game theory, developed by John Nash, offers insights into strategic decision-making and interaction, particularly in competitive environments. In strategic communication, game theory can be applied to anticipate and influence the responses of competitors, stakeholders, and audiences.
    - DEM can be integrated with game theory by using the Directive Mode to establish a strong initial position and the Exploratory Mode to adapt to the actions and reactions of others. For example, in a competitive market, a company might use the Directive Mode to launch a new product with a clear value proposition, then shift to the Exploratory Mode to gather feedback, monitor competitors' responses, and adjust its strategy

accordingly.

- **Behavioral Economics in Marketing (Thaler & Sunstein, 2008)**:
  - Behavioral economics explores how psychological factors influence decision-making, offering valuable insights for crafting messages that resonate with audiences. DEM can enhance behavioral economics strategies by providing a framework for balancing persuasive messaging (Directive Mode) with efforts to engage and motivate the audience (Exploratory Mode).
  - For example, in a marketing campaign for a new product, the Directive Mode might be used to present the product's key features and benefits, while the Exploratory Mode could involve interactive ads or social media campaigns that encourage consumer participation, feedback, and brand engagement.

Case Studies: DEM in Strategic Communication

To illustrate the practical application of DEM in strategic communication, this section presents several case studies from different industries and communication contexts.

- **Case Study 1: Crisis Communication in the Airline Industry**:
  - **Context**: An airline faces a public relations crisis following a major incident that results in widespread negative media coverage. The airline needs to quickly restore public trust and manage the fallout.
  - **Application of DEM**: The airline's communication team uses the Directive Mode to issue a clear, factual statement about the incident, outlining the steps being taken to address the situation and ensure passenger safety. The team then employs the Exploratory Mode to engage with customers on social media, respond to concerns, and provide real-time updates.
  - **Outcomes**: The combination of directive and exploratory

communication helps the airline manage the crisis effectively, restoring public confidence and minimizing reputational damage.

- **Case Study 2: Launching a New Technology Product**:

  - **Context**: A tech company prepares to launch a groundbreaking new product in a highly competitive market. The company aims to generate excitement and secure a strong market position.

  - **Application of DEM**: The company uses the Directive Mode to create a high-impact launch event, presenting the product's key features, benefits, and unique selling points. Following the launch, the company shifts to the Exploratory Mode, engaging with early adopters through online forums, social media, and user feedback sessions to refine the product and build a community of loyal customers.

  - **Outcomes**: The strategic use of DEM results in a successful product launch, with strong initial sales and positive buzz in the market. The ongoing engagement with customers also leads to valuable insights that inform future product development and marketing strategies.

- **Case Study 3: Public Health Campaign to Promote Vaccination**:

  - **Context**: A public health organization launches a campaign to increase vaccination rates in a community with low uptake. The campaign needs to overcome misinformation and build trust.

  - **Application of DEM**: The organization uses the Directive Mode to disseminate clear, evidence-based information about the safety and benefits of vaccination. The Exploratory Mode is used in community outreach efforts, where healthcare workers engage with residents, address their concerns, and provide personalized support for making informed decisions.

- **Outcomes**: The campaign successfully increases vaccination rates by combining authoritative messaging with empathetic, community-focused engagement. The use of DEM helps to build trust and overcome barriers to vaccination.

Future Research Directions in Strategic Communication and DEM

As the application of DEM in strategic communication continues to evolve, there are numerous opportunities for future research to further explore its impact and potential.

- **Research on the Efficacy of DEM in Different Communication Contexts**:
  - Future research could investigate the efficacy of DEM in various strategic communication contexts, including crisis communication, marketing, public relations, and political campaigns. Studies could explore how the balance of directive and exploratory communication influences audience engagement, message retention, and behavioral outcomes.
  - Comparative studies could also examine the effectiveness of DEM-based communication strategies compared to traditional approaches, providing insights into the unique benefits and challenges of using DEM in strategic communication.
- **Development of DEM-Based Communication Tools**:
  - There is potential for the development of communication tools and resources that support the use of DEM in strategic communication. These tools might include digital platforms, message development frameworks, and assessment tools that help communicators craft and deliver effective messages.
  - Research could focus on the development and validation of these tools, ensuring that they are effective in improving communication outcomes and enhancing audience

engagement.

- **Exploration of Cross-Cultural Applications of DEM in Strategic Communication:**
  - As DEM is applied in diverse cultural contexts, it is important to explore how its principles can be adapted to meet the needs of different audiences. Future research could investigate how DEM-based communication strategies can be tailored to respect and incorporate cultural values, beliefs, and communication norms, ensuring that they are both effective and culturally sensitive.

Conclusion

Chapter 14 has provided a comprehensive exploration of how the Dual-Mode Elicitation Model (DEM) can be applied in strategic communication to craft effective messages and engage diverse audiences. By integrating insights from communication theory, strategic communication frameworks, public relations models, Edward Bernays' principles of propaganda, game theory, and behavioral economics, this chapter has demonstrated the potential of DEM to shape public perception and influence behavior. The case studies presented offer practical examples of how DEM can be implemented in different communication contexts, while the discussion of future research directions highlights the ongoing potential for innovation in this field. As communicators continue to refine their use of DEM, its application in strategic communication holds great promise for achieving organizational objectives and influencing public opinion.

16.

DEM in Customer Relationship Management (CRM)

Introduction

In the rapidly evolving landscape of Customer Relationship Management (CRM), the ability to establish meaningful, personalized communication with customers is more critical than ever. The Dual-Mode Elicitation Model (DEM) offers a powerful framework for enhancing customer interactions, building loyalty, and fostering long-term relationships. This chapter explores how DEM can be effectively applied in CRM by integrating insights from consumer psychology, personalized marketing, and behavioral economics. The discussion draws on foundational theories such as Edward Bernays' work on propaganda, Tajfel and Turner's Social Identity Theory, and Thaler and Sunstein's research on behavioral economics.

CRM Strategies and DEM Integration

Customer Relationship Management (CRM) is centered on the development and maintenance of strong relationships with customers. Traditional CRM strategies have focused on segmentation, targeting, and positioning (STP) to manage customer interactions. However, the rise of digital communication channels and the availability of vast amounts of customer data have shifted the focus toward personalized communication. Here, DEM plays a pivotal role by offering a structured approach to eliciting customer needs and preferences, allowing for the creation of tailored communication strategies that resonate with individual customers.

Personalized Communication Strategies

Personalization in CRM involves tailoring communication and

marketing efforts to meet the specific needs and preferences of individual customers. DEM's Directive and Exploratory Modes can be strategically employed to enhance this personalization. The Directive Mode, which focuses on guiding the customer through a structured decision-making process, can be used to deliver targeted messages that align with the customer's known preferences. On the other hand, the Exploratory Mode can be leveraged to gather deeper insights into customer motivations and desires, allowing for more nuanced and flexible communication.

For instance, a CRM system that uses DEM might start by employing the Directive Mode to send personalized product recommendations based on a customer's purchase history. Subsequently, the Exploratory Mode could be used to engage the customer in a dialogue about their broader interests and future needs, thereby enabling the system to refine its recommendations over time.

Consumer Psychology and Bernays' Propaganda

Edward Bernays, often referred to as the father of public relations, introduced the concept of propaganda as a tool for influencing public opinion and consumer behavior (Bernays, 1928). His insights into the power of targeted messaging are directly relevant to CRM, where the goal is to influence customer perceptions and drive loyalty.

In the context of DEM, Bernays' principles can be applied through the Directive Mode, where communication is carefully crafted to shape customer perceptions. For example, a CRM strategy might involve creating content that emphasizes the exclusivity and high value of a product, thereby encouraging customers to perceive it as a premium offering. This approach not only drives sales but also enhances brand loyalty by reinforcing the customer's belief in the brand's superiority.

Social Identity Theory in CRM

Social Identity Theory, developed by Henri Tajfel and John Turner (1979), posits that individuals derive a sense of identity and self-esteem from their membership in social groups. In the realm of

CRM, this theory can be leveraged to foster a sense of belonging among customers, which in turn enhances loyalty.

DEM can facilitate this process by using the Exploratory Mode to identify the social groups or communities that a customer identifies with. For instance, a CRM system might engage a customer in a conversation about their hobbies, interests, and affiliations. This information can then be used to craft messages that align with the customer's social identity, such as marketing products that are popular within their social group or highlighting the brand's involvement in community events.

Behavioral Economics in Consumer Behavior

Behavioral economics, as explored by Thaler and Sunstein (2008), examines how psychological, cognitive, and emotional factors influence economic decisions. This field offers valuable insights for CRM, particularly in understanding how customers make purchasing decisions and how they can be nudged toward desired behaviors.

DEM's dual modes can be instrumental in applying behavioral economics principles within CRM. The Directive Mode can be used to create structured decision-making paths that guide customers toward purchasing decisions that are beneficial for both the customer and the company. For example, a CRM system might use default options (a concept from behavioral economics) to streamline the decision-making process, such as pre-selecting the most popular product configurations in a customer's shopping cart.

Conversely, the Exploratory Mode can be used to understand the underlying motivations and biases that drive customer behavior. By engaging customers in open-ended conversations, CRM systems can gather insights into their preferences and concerns, which can then be addressed through personalized offers or messages.

Case Studies and Practical Applications

To illustrate the practical application of DEM in CRM, consider the following case study:

Case Study: Luxury Fashion Brand

A luxury fashion brand implemented a CRM system based on DEM principles to enhance customer loyalty. The system employed the Directive Mode to send personalized recommendations based on customers' past purchases and browsing behavior. Additionally, the Exploratory Mode was used to engage customers in conversations about their lifestyle, fashion preferences, and social activities.

As a result, the brand was able to create highly targeted marketing campaigns that resonated with individual customers. For instance, customers who expressed an interest in sustainable fashion were targeted with personalized messages highlighting the brand's eco-friendly collections. This approach not only increased sales but also strengthened the emotional connection between the brand and its customers, leading to higher levels of customer loyalty.

Future Research Opportunities

While the application of DEM in CRM has shown promising results, there are several areas for future research. One area of interest is the integration of DEM with emerging technologies such as artificial intelligence (AI) and machine learning. These technologies could further enhance the personalization of CRM by enabling real-time analysis of customer interactions and the dynamic adjustment of communication strategies.

Additionally, future research could explore the long-term impact of DEM-based CRM strategies on customer loyalty and brand equity. By conducting longitudinal studies, researchers could assess how sustained use of DEM in CRM influences customer perceptions and behaviors over time.

Conclusion

The application of DEM in Customer Relationship Management represents a significant advancement in personalized communication strategies. By integrating insights from consumer psychology, social identity theory, and behavioral economics, DEM offers a comprehensive framework for enhancing customer interactions and building loyalty. As organizations continue to explore the potential of DEM in CRM, future research will be crucial in uncovering new opportunities for innovation and improvement.

17.

Personalizing Sales Strategies with DEM

Introduction

In today's competitive marketplace, personalized sales strategies are essential for meeting the unique needs and preferences of individual customers. The Dual-Mode Elicitation Model (DEM) offers a robust framework for tailoring sales approaches by balancing directive and exploratory communication modes. This chapter explores how DEM can be applied to personalize sales strategies, integrating insights from sales psychology, consumer behavior, personalized selling techniques, evolutionary psychology, and behavioral economics. Through practical advice and case studies, this chapter demonstrates how DEM can enhance sales effectiveness and customer satisfaction. Additionally, future research directions are suggested to further refine the application of DEM in sales.

Foundations of Personalized Sales Strategies and DEM

Personalized sales strategies involve understanding and addressing the specific needs, preferences, and behaviors of individual customers. DEM provides a structured approach to personalization by allowing sales professionals to adapt their communication style based on the customer's unique characteristics and decision-making processes.

- **Sales Psychology and Consumer Behavior (Cialdini, 2001; Kotler & Keller, 2012):**

    ◦ Sales psychology focuses on understanding the psychological factors that influence consumer behavior, such as motivation, perception, and attitudes. DEM aligns with sales psychology by providing a framework for tailoring communication to the customer's psychological profile, ensuring that sales messages resonate on a deeper level.

- ◦ Consumer behavior research highlights the importance of understanding the buyer's journey, including the stages of need recognition, information search, evaluation of alternatives, purchase decision, and post-purchase behavior. DEM supports this understanding by offering a flexible approach to guiding customers through each stage of the buying process, using directive communication to provide clear information and exploratory communication to address concerns and build relationships.

- **Personalized Selling Techniques (Zoltners et al., 2006):**

  - ◦ Personalized selling involves customizing the sales approach to meet the specific needs and preferences of each customer. Techniques such as consultative selling, relationship selling, and solution selling are all forms of personalized selling that can be enhanced by DEM.
  - ◦ The Directive Mode in DEM is used to deliver clear, personalized information that addresses the customer's specific needs, while the Exploratory Mode encourages open-ended dialogue, allowing the salesperson to uncover additional insights and tailor their approach further.

Integrating Evolutionary Psychology into DEM-Based Sales Strategies

Evolutionary psychology provides insights into the deep-seated psychological drivers that influence decision-making, such as the need for safety, social belonging, and status. Understanding these drivers can help sales professionals tailor their approaches to align with customers' innate tendencies.

- **Evolutionary Psychology's Role in Decision-Making (Cosmides & Tooby, 1992):**

  - ◦ Evolutionary psychology suggests that human decision-making is influenced by evolved cognitive mechanisms that have been shaped by the challenges of survival and reproduction. These mechanisms include risk aversion, preference for social proof, and sensitivity to reciprocity.

  - DEM can be applied to leverage these evolutionary drivers in sales. For example, the Directive Mode can be used to provide clear, authoritative information that reduces perceived risk, while the Exploratory Mode can engage the customer in a dialogue that builds trust and leverages social proof.

- **Applying Evolutionary Psychology to Personalize Sales**:

  - Sales professionals can use DEM to personalize their approach by recognizing and responding to the evolutionary drivers that influence their customers' decisions. For example, a customer who is motivated by status may respond positively to messaging that highlights the exclusivity and prestige of a product (Directive Mode), followed by an exploratory discussion that reinforces the social benefits of ownership.

  - Similarly, customers who are risk-averse may require more detailed information and reassurance before making a purchase. The salesperson can use the Directive Mode to provide clear, factual information that addresses the customer's concerns, and the Exploratory Mode to engage the customer in a discussion about their specific needs and how the product or service can meet those needs.

Behavioral Economics and DEM in Sales

Behavioral economics explores how psychological factors influence economic decision-making, offering valuable insights for crafting personalized sales strategies. DEM enhances the application of behavioral economics in sales by providing a framework for balancing persuasive messaging with customer engagement.

- **Behavioral Economics in Sales (Thaler & Sunstein, 2008)**:
    - Behavioral economics principles, such as nudging and framing, can be used to influence customer decisions by presenting choices in a way that guides them toward a desired outcome. DEM supports these principles by offering a structured approach to delivering persuasive messages (Directive Mode) while also allowing for customer engagement and feedback (Exploratory Mode).
    - For example, in a sales context, the Directive Mode might be used to frame a product as the best choice based on the customer's specific needs and preferences. The Exploratory Mode can then be used to engage the customer in a discussion about how the product fits into their life or solves a particular problem, increasing the likelihood of a purchase.
- **Using DEM to Influence Decision-Making**:
    - Sales professionals can use DEM to influence decision-making by combining clear, persuasive messaging with opportunities for the customer to explore their options and make informed choices. This approach helps to build trust and rapport, leading to more successful sales outcomes.
    - For instance, a salesperson might use the Directive Mode to present a limited-time offer, creating a sense of urgency and framing the product as a valuable opportunity. The Exploratory Mode can then be used to address any hesitations the customer may have, explore alternative options, and reinforce the benefits of making a timely decision.

Case Studies: DEM in Personalized Sales Strategies

To illustrate the practical application of DEM in personalized sales strategies, this section presents several case studies from different industries.

- **Case Study 1: Tailoring Sales in the Luxury Goods Market**:
    - **Context**: A luxury car dealership seeks to enhance its sales approach by personalizing interactions with high-net-worth customers.
    - **Application of DEM**: The sales team uses the Directive Mode to provide detailed information about the features and benefits of each vehicle, tailored to the customer's lifestyle and preferences. The Exploratory Mode is used during test drives and consultations to engage customers in discussions about their personal tastes, driving habits, and long-term goals.
    - **Outcomes**: The personalized approach leads to higher customer satisfaction and increased sales, as customers feel that their unique needs and preferences are being understood and met. The use of DEM helps the dealership build long-term relationships with customers, leading to repeat business and referrals.
- **Case Study 2: Personalized Sales in the Technology Sector**:
    - **Context**: A software company seeks to increase sales by tailoring its approach to small and medium-sized enterprises (SMEs) with diverse needs and budgets.
    - **Application of DEM**: The sales team uses the Directive Mode to present customized software packages that address the specific challenges faced by each SME. The Exploratory Mode is used during consultations to understand the unique business processes, pain points, and growth aspirations of each client, allowing the sales team to offer tailored solutions.
    - **Outcomes**: The DEM-based approach results in higher conversion rates and stronger client relationships, as the tailored solutions directly address the needs of each SME. The company also gains valuable insights into the challenges and opportunities within the SME market, informing future product development and sales

strategies.

- **Case Study 3: DEM in Retail Sales**:
  - **Context**: A retail chain seeks to improve customer experience and increase sales by personalizing in-store interactions.
  - **Application of DEM**: Retail associates are trained to use the Directive Mode to provide clear, informative guidance on product features, availability, and pricing. The Exploratory Mode is used to engage customers in conversations about their personal style, preferences, and shopping goals, helping associates recommend products that align with the customer's individual tastes.
  - **Outcomes**: The personalized sales approach leads to higher customer satisfaction, increased sales, and greater customer loyalty. The use of DEM helps the retail chain differentiate itself in a competitive market by offering a superior, personalized shopping experience.

Practical Tools and Methodologies for Implementing DEM in Sales

To effectively implement DEM in sales strategies, sales professionals need practical tools and methodologies that support its integration into their sales processes.

- **Developing DEM-Based Sales Training Programs**:
  - Sales organizations can develop training programs that teach sales professionals how to apply DEM principles in their interactions with customers. These programs should include modules on understanding customer psychology, tailoring communication to individual needs, and using both directive and exploratory communication modes effectively.
  - Training can be delivered through workshops, role-playing exercises, and real-world scenarios, allowing sales professionals to practice and refine their use of DEM in a supportive environment.

- **Using Technology to Support DEM in Sales**:
    - CRM (Customer Relationship Management) systems can be enhanced with DEM principles, allowing sales professionals to track and analyze customer interactions, preferences, and feedback. This data can inform personalized sales strategies, ensuring that each customer receives the right balance of directive and exploratory communication.
    - AI-powered sales tools can also be developed to support DEM-based sales strategies. These tools could use machine learning to analyze customer behavior and preferences, offering sales professionals real-time recommendations for tailoring their approach.
- **Creating a Culture of Personalization with DEM**:
    - Sales organizations can promote a culture of personalization by encouraging the use of DEM across all sales interactions. This might involve incorporating DEM principles into organizational policies, performance evaluations, and incentive programs, as well as recognizing and rewarding sales professionals who excel at personalizing their sales approach.
    - Ongoing support and resources should be provided to help sales professionals refine their use of DEM, including access to mentorship, continuing education opportunities, and peer support networks.

Future Research Directions in DEM and Sales

As the application of DEM in sales continues to evolve, there are numerous opportunities for future research to further explore its impact and potential.

- **Research on the Efficacy of DEM in Different Sales Contexts**:
    - Future research could investigate the efficacy of DEM in various sales contexts, including B2B (business-to-

business), B2C (business-to-consumer), and direct sales. Studies could explore how the balance of directive and exploratory communication influences sales outcomes, customer satisfaction, and long-term customer relationships.

  ◦ Comparative studies could also examine the effectiveness of DEM-based sales strategies compared to traditional approaches, providing insights into the unique benefits and challenges of using DEM in sales.

- **Development of DEM-Based Sales Tools:**

  ◦ There is potential for the development of sales tools and resources that support the use of DEM in personalized sales strategies. These tools might include digital platforms, sales scripts, and assessment tools that help sales professionals implement DEM in their practice.

  ◦ Research could focus on the development and validation of these tools, ensuring that they are effective in improving sales outcomes and enhancing customer satisfaction.

- **Exploration of Cross-Cultural Applications of DEM in Sales:**

  ◦ As DEM is applied in diverse sales contexts around the world, it is important to explore how its principles can be adapted to meet the needs of different cultural and customer groups. Future research could investigate how DEM-based sales strategies can be tailored to respect and incorporate cultural values, beliefs, and communication norms, ensuring that they are both effective and culturally sensitive.

Conclusion

Chapter 16 has provided a comprehensive exploration of how the Dual-Mode Elicitation Model (DEM) can be applied to personalize sales strategies, tailoring approaches to individual customers and enhancing sales effectiveness. By integrating insights from sales psychology, consumer behavior, personalized selling techniques, evolutionary psychology, and behavioral economics, this chapter has demonstrated the potential of DEM to transform sales practices and improve customer satisfaction. The case studies presented offer practical examples of how DEM can be implemented in different sales contexts, while the discussion of practical tools and future research directions highlights the ongoing potential for innovation in this field. As sales professionals continue to refine their use of DEM, its application in personalized sales strategies holds great promise for achieving sales success and building lasting customer relationships.

18.

The Ethical Implications of DEM

Introduction

The Dual-Mode Elicitation Model (DEM) offers a versatile framework for optimizing communication across various fields, including AI, healthcare, and strategic communication. However, the application of DEM also raises significant ethical considerations that must be addressed to ensure its responsible use. This chapter explores the ethical implications of DEM, drawing on insights from AI ethics, bioethics, communication ethics, and philosophical frameworks. Through a detailed analysis of potential ethical challenges and guidelines for responsible implementation, this chapter aims to provide a comprehensive framework for ethical decision-making in the use of DEM. Additionally, future research directions are suggested to further explore and refine the ethical dimensions of DEM.

Ethical Challenges in the Application of DEM

The application of DEM across different fields introduces several ethical challenges that require careful consideration. These challenges are particularly relevant in contexts where miscommunication, manipulation, or mental health impacts are possible.

- **AI Ethics (Dignum, 2018):**
    - The integration of DEM into AI systems, particularly in areas like customer service, healthcare, and autonomous decision-making, raises ethical questions about transparency, accountability, and the potential for manipulation. AI systems that use DEM to engage with users must be designed to prioritize ethical

considerations, such as ensuring that users are fully informed about the AI's capabilities and limitations.

  - There is also a need to address the potential for bias in AI systems that use DEM. Bias in AI can lead to unfair or discriminatory outcomes, particularly when the AI is used in decision-making processes that affect individuals' lives. Ethical guidelines must be established to ensure that AI systems using DEM are designed and deployed in ways that minimize bias and promote fairness.

- **Bioethics in Healthcare (Beauchamp & Childress, 2013):**

  - In healthcare, the application of DEM can enhance patient-centered care, but it also introduces ethical concerns related to patient autonomy, informed consent, and the potential for coercion. Healthcare providers must ensure that the use of DEM in patient interactions respects patients' autonomy and supports informed decision-making without exerting undue influence.

  - Additionally, the use of DEM in healthcare must consider the potential for miscommunication, particularly in situations where patients may have limited health literacy or face language barriers. Ethical guidelines should be established to ensure that communication using DEM is clear, accurate, and tailored to the patient's needs and abilities.

- **Communication Ethics (Johannesen, 2002):**

  - The application of DEM in strategic communication, marketing, and public relations raises ethical questions about honesty, transparency, and the potential for manipulation. Communicators using DEM must be mindful of the ethical implications of their messaging, particularly when it comes to balancing persuasive intent with the need for transparency and truthfulness.

  - Ethical considerations also extend to the potential impact of DEM on public perception and trust. Communicators must be careful not to use DEM in ways that exploit audiences' vulnerabilities or mislead them about the nature or purpose of the communication.

Ethical Frameworks for Evaluating DEM

To address the ethical challenges associated with DEM, it is essential to draw on established ethical frameworks that provide guidance for responsible decision-making.

- **Wendell Johnson's *People in Quandaries* (Johnson, 1946):**
  - Wendell Johnson's work in general semantics highlights the ethical implications of language use and the potential for miscommunication to create confusion, conflict, and harm. In the context of DEM, Johnson's insights underscore the importance of clear, accurate communication that respects the audience's ability to understand and engage with the message.
  - Ethical communication using DEM should prioritize clarity, transparency, and respect for the audience's autonomy. Communicators must be aware of the potential for language to shape perceptions and influence behavior, and they should strive to use DEM in ways that promote understanding and empowerment rather than manipulation or coercion.
- **Immanuel Kant's Deontological Ethics (Kant, 1785/1996):**
  - Immanuel Kant's deontological ethics emphasizes the importance of acting according to moral principles that respect the dignity and autonomy of individuals. In the context of DEM, Kant's framework provides a basis for evaluating the ethical implications of communication strategies, particularly when it comes to respecting the rights and autonomy of the audience.
  - Kant's categorical imperative, which states that one should act only according to maxims that could be universally applied, offers a valuable guideline for the use of DEM.

Communicators should ensure that their use of DEM is guided by principles that could be universally endorsed, such as honesty, transparency, and respect for autonomy.

- **Ethics of Autonomous Decision-Making (Lin, 2016)**:
  - The use of DEM in AI systems, particularly those involving autonomous decision-making, raises ethical questions about responsibility, accountability, and the potential for harm. Patrick Lin's work on the ethics of autonomous systems highlights the importance of ensuring that AI systems are designed and operated in ways that prioritize human well-being and minimize the risk of harm.
  - In the context of DEM, ethical considerations include ensuring that AI systems are transparent about their decision-making processes, that they are designed to avoid bias and discrimination, and that they include safeguards to prevent unintended consequences.

Phenomenological Control and Ethical Considerations

Phenomenological control refers to the ability to influence one's subjective experiences, and it has significant ethical implications in the context of DEM, particularly when it comes to the potential for manipulation or coercion.

- **Phenomenological Control in Communication (Carhart-Harris et al., 2014)**:
  - The use of phenomenological control in communication involves guiding the audience's attention, perceptions, and interpretations in ways that can shape their subjective experience of the message. While this can be a powerful tool for enhancing communication effectiveness, it also raises ethical concerns about the potential for manipulation or undue influence.
  - Ethical use of phenomenological control with DEM requires a commitment to transparency and respect for the audience's autonomy. Communicators should avoid

using phenomenological control in ways that exploit vulnerabilities or manipulate the audience's perceptions without their awareness or consent.

- **Ethical Guidelines for Using Phenomenological Control**:
  - To ensure that phenomenological control is used ethically with DEM, communicators should adhere to guidelines that prioritize the audience's well-being and autonomy. This includes providing clear information about the nature and purpose of the communication, avoiding deceptive or coercive tactics, and ensuring that the audience has the opportunity to make informed choices about their engagement with the message.
  - Additionally, communicators should be mindful of the potential for unintended consequences, such as the reinforcement of harmful beliefs or behaviors, and take steps to mitigate these risks.

Developing a Comprehensive Ethical Framework for DEM

To guide the responsible use of DEM, it is essential to develop a comprehensive ethical framework that addresses the specific challenges and considerations associated with its application.

- **Guidelines for Ethical Use of DEM**:
  - The ethical framework for DEM should include guidelines that address the following key considerations:
    - **Transparency**: Ensure that the audience is fully informed about the nature and purpose of the communication, including the use of DEM.
    - **Autonomy**: Respect the audience's right to make informed decisions about their engagement with the message, avoiding coercive or manipulative tactics.
    - **Accountability**: Establish clear lines of responsibility for the use of DEM, particularly in contexts where it may have significant impacts on individuals or

communities.

- **Fairness**: Ensure that the use of DEM is free from bias and discrimination, and that it promotes equitable outcomes for all individuals.
- **Well-being**: Prioritize the well-being of the audience, avoiding communication strategies that could cause harm or distress.

- **Implementing Ethical Guidelines in Practice**:

  - To implement these guidelines in practice, organizations using DEM should develop and enforce policies that promote ethical communication. This might include training programs for communicators, regular ethical audits of communication practices, and mechanisms for addressing ethical concerns or violations.
  - Additionally, organizations should engage in ongoing dialogue with stakeholders, including the audience, to ensure that their use of DEM aligns with ethical principles and addresses any emerging concerns.

Case Studies: Ethical Implications of DEM in Practice

To illustrate the ethical implications of DEM in practice, this section presents several case studies from different fields.

- **Case Study 1: Ethical Use of DEM in AI-Powered Customer Service**:

  - **Context**: A company uses DEM to develop an AI-powered customer service chatbot that interacts with customers and resolves their inquiries. The chatbot uses both directive and exploratory modes to engage with customers and provide personalized support.
  - **Ethical Considerations**: The company faces ethical challenges related to transparency, bias, and accountability. To address these challenges, the company implements ethical guidelines that ensure customers are

informed about the chatbot's AI nature, that the chatbot is designed to avoid biased responses, and that human oversight is available to address complex issues.

  - **Outcomes**: The ethical use of DEM in the chatbot's design and operation leads to high levels of customer satisfaction and trust, while minimizing the risk of ethical violations.

- **Case Study 2: Ethical Challenges in Healthcare Communication with DEM**:

  - **Context**: A healthcare provider uses DEM to enhance patient communication, particularly in the context of delivering difficult diagnoses. The provider uses directive communication to explain the diagnosis clearly and exploratory communication to engage with the patient's emotions and concerns.

  - **Ethical Considerations**: The provider must navigate ethical challenges related to patient autonomy, informed consent, and emotional well-being. The provider follows ethical guidelines that ensure the patient is fully informed about their condition and treatment options, that their autonomy is respected, and that their emotional needs are addressed with sensitivity.

  - **Outcomes**: The ethical application of DEM in patient communication leads to improved patient outcomes, including greater understanding, satisfaction, and emotional support.

- **Case Study 3: Ethical Implications of DEM in Political Communication**:

  - **Context**: A political campaign uses DEM to craft messages that resonate with voters, balancing directive communication of policy positions with exploratory engagement with voter concerns.

  - **Ethical Considerations**: The campaign must address ethical challenges related to transparency, truthfulness, and the potential for manipulation. The campaign implements ethical guidelines that ensure all messaging is factually accurate, that voters are fully informed about the candidate's positions, and that communication strategies avoid exploiting voter emotions or fears.

- **Outcomes**: The ethical use of DEM in the campaign contributes to a positive public perception of the candidate, fostering trust and engagement without resorting to manipulative tactics.

Future Research Directions in Ethical Implications of DEM

As the application of DEM continues to evolve, there are numerous opportunities for future research to further explore its ethical implications.

- **Research on Ethical Implications of DEM in Emerging Technologies:**

  - Future research could investigate the ethical implications of DEM in emerging technologies, such as AI, virtual reality, and augmented reality. Studies could explore how the integration of DEM into these technologies raises new ethical challenges and how these challenges can be addressed through ethical guidelines and regulatory frameworks.

- **Development of Ethical Decision-Making Models for DEM:**

  - There is potential for the development of ethical decision-making models specifically designed for the use of DEM. These models could provide communicators and organizations with tools for evaluating the ethical implications of their use of DEM, ensuring that they make informed and responsible decisions.

- **Exploration of Cross-Cultural Ethical Considerations in DEM:**

  - As DEM is applied in diverse cultural contexts, it is important to explore the ethical implications of its use across different cultural and social settings. Future research could investigate how ethical considerations related to DEM vary across cultures and how ethical guidelines can be adapted to respect and incorporate cultural values and norms.

Conclusion

Chapter 17 has provided a comprehensive exploration of the ethical implications of the Dual-Mode Elicitation Model (DEM), addressing the challenges and considerations associated with its application across different fields. By integrating insights from AI ethics, bioethics, communication ethics, and philosophical frameworks, this chapter has demonstrated the importance of developing and implementing ethical guidelines for the responsible use of DEM. The case studies presented offer practical examples of how ethical considerations can be addressed in different contexts, while the discussion of future research directions highlights the ongoing potential for exploring and refining the ethical dimensions of DEM. As organizations and communicators continue to apply DEM, it is essential that they prioritize ethical decision-making to ensure that its use promotes fairness, transparency, and the well-being of all individuals.

19.

Cross-Cultural Communication with DEM

Introduction

In an increasingly globalized world, effective cross-cultural communication is essential for fostering understanding, collaboration, and success across diverse settings. The Dual-Mode Elicitation Model (DEM) offers a flexible framework for enhancing communication across cultures by adapting its principles to address the unique challenges of intercultural interactions. This chapter explores how DEM can be adapted for cross-cultural communication, integrating insights from intercultural communication theory, global communication strategies, cultural psychology, interpretive anthropology, Social Identity Theory, and ecological psychology. Through case studies and practical strategies, this chapter provides a comprehensive guide to using DEM in diverse cultural contexts. Additionally, future research directions are suggested to further refine the application of DEM in cross-cultural communication.

Foundations of Cross-Cultural Communication and DEM

Cross-cultural communication involves navigating the complexities of interacting with individuals from different cultural backgrounds, each with their own values, norms, and communication styles. DEM provides a versatile framework for adapting communication strategies to these diverse contexts, enhancing understanding and reducing the potential for miscommunication.

- **Intercultural Communication Theory (Gudykunst & Kim, 2003):**

  - Intercultural communication theory explores the ways in

which cultural differences impact communication, emphasizing the importance of cultural awareness, empathy, and adaptability. DEM aligns with these principles by offering a model that can be tailored to the specific cultural context, ensuring that communication is both effective and respectful.

  ○ In cross-cultural interactions, the Directive Mode in DEM can be used to provide clear, structured communication that minimizes ambiguity, while the Exploratory Mode encourages open-ended dialogue that allows for the exploration of cultural nuances and the building of mutual understanding.

- **Global Communication Strategies (Neuliep, 2014)**:

  ○ Global communication strategies involve the development of communication practices that are effective across different cultural settings. These strategies often require a balance between consistency in messaging and adaptation to local cultural norms.

  ○ DEM supports global communication strategies by providing a framework for balancing directive communication, which ensures consistency and clarity, with exploratory communication, which allows for the adaptation of messages to align with local cultural values and expectations.

Adapting DEM for Cross-Cultural Communication

Adapting DEM for cross-cultural communication involves recognizing and addressing the specific cultural factors that influence how messages are received and interpreted. This requires an understanding of cultural psychology, interpretive anthropology, and Social Identity Theory.

- **Cultural Psychology and Communication (Markus & Kitayama, 1991)**:

  ○ Cultural psychology examines how cultural contexts shape

psychological processes, including communication. Different cultures have distinct communication styles, values, and norms that influence how messages are conveyed and understood.

- ○ DEM can be adapted to cultural psychology by adjusting the balance of directive and exploratory communication based on the cultural context. For example, in high-context cultures where communication is often indirect and relies heavily on non-verbal cues, the Exploratory Mode may be more prominent, allowing for the subtle negotiation of meaning. In contrast, low-context cultures may require more directive communication to ensure that the message is explicit and clear.

- **Clifford Geertz's Interpretive Anthropology (Geertz, 1973):**

  - ○ Clifford Geertz's interpretive anthropology emphasizes the importance of understanding culture as a system of meanings that individuals use to make sense of the world. This perspective highlights the need for communicators to be attuned to the cultural meanings that influence how messages are interpreted.

  - ○ In the context of DEM, interpretive anthropology can inform the adaptation of communication strategies by providing insights into the symbolic and contextual elements of culture that shape communication. Communicators can use the Exploratory Mode to engage with these cultural meanings, allowing for a deeper understanding of the audience's perspective and facilitating more meaningful interactions.

- **Social Identity Theory (Tajfel & Turner, 1979):**

  - ○ Social Identity Theory explores how individuals' sense of identity is influenced by their membership in social groups, including cultural groups. This theory highlights the importance of recognizing and addressing the social identities that influence communication in cross-cultural contexts.

- ○ DEM can be adapted to Social Identity Theory by incorporating strategies that acknowledge and respect the social identities of the audience. For example, communicators can use the Exploratory Mode to engage in dialogue that affirms the audience's cultural identity, while the Directive Mode can be used to provide information that is relevant to the audience's social context.

Ecological Psychology and DEM in Varying Environments

Ecological psychology, which focuses on the relationship between individuals and their environments, offers valuable insights for adapting DEM to different cultural contexts. By considering the affordances and constraints of the environment, communicators can tailor their strategies to better align with the cultural context.

- **Ecological Psychology (Gibson, 1979)**:
  - ○ James Gibson's work on affordances in ecological psychology emphasizes the ways in which the environment provides opportunities for action and influences behavior. In communication, the cultural environment can be seen as providing affordances that shape how messages are received and interpreted.
  - ○ DEM can be adapted to ecological psychology by considering the environmental factors that influence communication in different cultural settings. For example, in cultures where face-to-face communication is highly valued, the Exploratory Mode may be more effective in fostering engagement and building relationships. In contrast, in cultures where written communication is more prevalent, the Directive Mode may be used to ensure clarity and precision.
- **Applying Ecological Psychology to Cross-Cultural Communication**:

- Communicators can apply ecological psychology to DEM by assessing the cultural environment and identifying the affordances that are most relevant to the audience. This might involve considering factors such as the preferred communication channels, the role of technology in communication, and the cultural norms that influence how messages are interpreted.
- By aligning DEM with the environmental affordances of the cultural context, communicators can enhance the effectiveness of their messages and reduce the potential for miscommunication.

Case Studies: DEM in Cross-Cultural Communication

To illustrate the practical application of DEM in cross-cultural communication, this section presents several case studies from different cultural contexts.

- **Case Study 1: Adapting Marketing Strategies for a Global Audience**:
  - **Context**: A multinational corporation seeks to launch a new product in multiple countries, each with its own cultural norms and communication styles.
  - **Application of DEM**: The marketing team uses the Directive Mode to ensure consistency in the core message across all markets, while the Exploratory Mode is adapted for each cultural context. In high-context cultures, the Exploratory Mode emphasizes storytelling and relationship-building, while in low-context cultures, it focuses on providing clear, direct information.
  - **Outcomes**: The adapted communication strategy leads to successful product launches across diverse markets, with positive consumer reception and strong brand engagement. The use of DEM helps the company navigate cultural differences and tailor its approach to meet the needs of each audience.

- **Case Study 2: Cross-Cultural Communication in International Diplomacy**:
  - **Context**: A government agency engages in diplomatic negotiations with representatives from multiple countries, each with its own cultural norms and expectations.
  - **Application of DEM**: The diplomatic team uses the Directive Mode to communicate the agency's official positions and policies, ensuring that key messages are clear and consistent. The Exploratory Mode is used in bilateral meetings to engage with the cultural perspectives of each country's representatives, fostering mutual understanding and cooperation.
  - **Outcomes**: The use of DEM in cross-cultural diplomacy enhances the effectiveness of negotiations, leading to successful agreements and stronger diplomatic relationships. The adapted communication strategy allows the agency to balance its own objectives with the need to respect and engage with the cultural values of its counterparts.
- **Case Study 3: Implementing Cross-Cultural Training Programs for Global Teams**:
  - **Context**: A global corporation implements cross-cultural training programs to enhance communication and collaboration among its diverse workforce.
  - **Application of DEM**: The training program uses the Directive Mode to provide clear guidelines and best practices for cross-cultural communication, while the Exploratory Mode encourages participants to share their own cultural experiences and perspectives. This approach allows the program to address common challenges while also fostering a deeper understanding of cultural differences.
  - **Outcomes**: The cross-cultural training program leads to improved communication and collaboration across the

corporation's global teams. Employees report greater cultural awareness and sensitivity, resulting in a more inclusive and effective work environment.

Practical Tools and Methodologies for Implementing DEM in Cross-Cultural Communication

To effectively implement DEM in cross-cultural communication, organizations and communicators need practical tools and methodologies that support its adaptation to diverse cultural contexts.

- **Developing Cross-Cultural Communication Guidelines with DEM**:
    - Organizations can develop communication guidelines that incorporate DEM principles, providing clear strategies for adapting communication to different cultural contexts. These guidelines should include examples of how to balance directive and exploratory communication based on cultural norms, as well as tips for recognizing and addressing cultural differences.
    - Training programs can be designed to help communicators develop the skills necessary to implement DEM in cross-cultural interactions, including cultural awareness training, role-playing exercises, and feedback sessions.
- **Using Technology to Support Cross-Cultural Communication with DEM**:
    - Digital tools and platforms can be developed to support the use of DEM in cross-cultural communication. For example, communication apps could be designed to provide real-time cultural insights and suggestions for adapting communication strategies based on the audience's cultural background.
    - AI-powered communication tools could also be developed to support cross-cultural interactions, offering features

that guide communicators in balancing directive and
exploratory modes based on the cultural context.

- **Creating a Culture of Cross-Cultural Communication with DEM:**
  - Organizations can promote a culture of cross-cultural communication by encouraging the use of DEM across all levels of communication. This might involve incorporating DEM principles into organizational policies, training programs, and performance evaluations, as well as recognizing and rewarding communicators who excel at adapting their strategies to diverse cultural contexts.
  - Ongoing support and resources should be provided to help communicators refine their use of DEM in cross-cultural settings, including access to cultural advisors, continuing education opportunities, and peer support networks.

Future Research Directions in Cross-Cultural Communication and DEM

As the application of DEM in cross-cultural communication continues to evolve, there are numerous opportunities for future research to further explore its impact and potential.

- **Research on the Efficacy of DEM in Different Cultural Contexts:**
  - Future research could investigate the efficacy of DEM in various cultural contexts, exploring how the balance of directive and exploratory communication influences communication outcomes across different cultures. Studies could examine how DEM can be adapted to specific cultural norms, values, and communication styles, providing insights into the most effective strategies for cross-cultural communication.
  - Comparative studies could also examine the effectiveness of DEM-based communication strategies compared to traditional approaches, offering a deeper understanding of

the unique benefits and challenges of using DEM in cross-cultural settings.

- **Development of Cross-Cultural Communication Tools with DEM:**
  - There is potential for the development of communication tools and resources that support the use of DEM in cross-cultural communication. These tools might include digital platforms, communication templates, and assessment tools that help communicators implement DEM in their practice.
  - Research could focus on the development and validation of these tools, ensuring that they are effective in enhancing cross-cultural communication and reducing the potential for miscommunication.
- **Exploration of Cross-Cultural Ethical Considerations in DEM:**
  - As DEM is applied in diverse cultural contexts, it is important to explore the ethical implications of its use across different cultures. Future research could investigate how ethical considerations related to DEM vary across cultures and how ethical guidelines can be adapted to respect and incorporate cultural values and norms.

Conclusion

Chapter 18 has provided a comprehensive exploration of how the Dual-Mode Elicitation Model (DEM) can be adapted for cross-cultural communication, addressing the challenges and opportunities associated with communicating across diverse cultural contexts. By integrating insights from intercultural communication theory, global communication strategies, cultural psychology, interpretive anthropology, Social Identity Theory, and ecological psychology, this chapter has demonstrated the potential of DEM to enhance cross-cultural understanding and reduce the potential for miscommunication. The case studies presented offer practical examples of how DEM can be implemented in different cultural settings, while the discussion of practical tools and future research directions highlights the ongoing potential for innovation in this field. As communicators continue to apply DEM in cross-cultural contexts, its application holds great promise for fostering understanding, collaboration, and success in an increasingly interconnected world.

20.

The Future of DEM in Communication Technologies

Introduction

As communication technologies continue to evolve, the Dual-Mode Elicitation Model (DEM) is poised to play a significant role in shaping the future of human interaction with emerging technologies. From virtual and augmented reality (VR/AR) to artificial intelligence (AI), the application of DEM in these domains promises to enhance the adaptability, effectiveness, and ethical considerations of communication systems. This chapter explores the potential impact of DEM on future communication technologies, focusing on cybernetic principles, adaptive systems, embodied cognition, and quantum decision-making. Additionally, it considers the speculative intersections of DEM with consciousness studies and phenomenological control, particularly in VR/AR environments. Through scenarios and case studies, this chapter illustrates possible future applications of DEM and concludes with research opportunities for advancing DEM in technology and exploring the frontiers of AI, consciousness, and transpersonal psychology.

Emerging Trends in Communication Technologies and DEM

The landscape of communication technologies is rapidly changing, driven by advancements in AI, VR/AR, and neuromemristive systems. These technologies offer new opportunities for enhancing human interaction and communication through DEM.

- **Future Communication Trends (Kaku, 2011):**

- Communication technologies are increasingly moving
  towards greater interactivity, personalization, and
  immersion. DEM is well-positioned to contribute to these
  trends by offering a framework that can be adapted to the
  dynamic and interactive nature of future communication
  systems.
- For example, in future AI-driven communication
  platforms, DEM could enable more personalized and
  responsive interactions, where the system dynamically
  adjusts its communication style based on the user's needs
  and preferences. This adaptability would enhance user
  engagement and satisfaction, making communication
  systems more intuitive and effective.

- **VR/AR in Communication (Lanier, 2017):**
  - Virtual and augmented reality technologies are
    transforming how we experience and interact with digital
    content. DEM can be applied to VR/AR environments to
    create more immersive and adaptive communication
    experiences.
  - In VR/AR, DEM could be used to enhance the realism and
    emotional impact of virtual interactions by enabling
    systems to switch between directive and exploratory
    communication modes based on the user's actions and
    responses. This would create a more natural and engaging
    experience, where the technology adapts to the user's
    needs in real-time.

- **Neuromemristive Systems (Mead, 2020):**
  - Neuromemristive systems, which mimic the neural
    processes of the human brain, offer the potential for more
    advanced and adaptive communication technologies. DEM
    could be integrated into these systems to enable more
    human-like communication capabilities in AI.
  - By leveraging the neuroplasticity of memristive systems,
    DEM could facilitate communication technologies that

learn and adapt over time, becoming more attuned to individual users' communication styles and preferences. This would enhance the system's ability to engage in meaningful and personalized interactions.

Cybernetic Principles and Adaptive Communication Systems

The application of cybernetic principles to communication technologies offers a framework for creating adaptive systems that can respond to the complexity and variability of human communication.

- **Norbert Wiener's Cybernetics (Wiener, 1948):**
  - Norbert Wiener's work on cybernetics laid the foundation for understanding systems that can self-regulate and adapt to changing conditions. DEM aligns with these principles by offering a model that can be integrated into adaptive communication systems, enabling them to respond dynamically to user input.
  - In future communication technologies, DEM could be used to create systems that continuously monitor and adjust their communication strategies based on real-time feedback. For example, an AI-powered customer service system could use DEM to adapt its communication style based on the user's emotional state, providing a more personalized and effective interaction.
- **Stafford Beer's Cybernetics and Management (Beer, 1972):**
  - Stafford Beer extended cybernetic principles to the management of complex systems, emphasizing the importance of adaptability and self-regulation. DEM could be applied in this context to create communication systems that are capable of managing complex interactions across multiple channels and contexts.
  - In a corporate setting, DEM could be used to develop communication platforms that adapt to the needs of different teams and departments, facilitating more

efficient and effective collaboration. These systems could dynamically switch between directive and exploratory modes based on the specific requirements of each communication task, enhancing productivity and decision-making.

Embodied Cognition and Communication Technologies

Embodied cognition, which emphasizes the role of the body in shaping the mind, offers valuable insights for developing communication technologies that are more intuitive and human-like.

- **Embodied Cognition in Communication (Gallagher, 2005):**
  - Embodied cognition suggests that our cognitive processes are deeply influenced by our physical bodies and interactions with the environment. DEM can be applied to communication technologies to create systems that are more attuned to the user's embodied experience.
  - In VR/AR environments, DEM could be used to create more immersive and responsive interactions by integrating sensory feedback and physical actions into the communication process. For example, a VR-based training program could use DEM to adapt its instructional methods based on the user's movements and physiological responses, creating a more effective and engaging learning experience.
- **Application of Embodied Cognition in AI (Wilson, 2002):**
  - AI systems that incorporate principles of embodied cognition can create more natural and intuitive interactions with users. DEM could be used to enhance these systems by enabling them to adapt their communication strategies based on the user's physical and emotional state.
  - For example, a healthcare AI system could use DEM to adjust its communication style based on the patient's

posture, tone of voice, and facial expressions, providing more personalized and empathetic care. This would create a more human-like interaction that builds trust and rapport with the patient.

Quantum Cognition and Decision Theory in DEM

Quantum cognition and decision theory offer a new perspective on how humans make decisions and process information, which can inform the development of more sophisticated communication technologies.

- **Quantum Cognition and Decision Theory (Busemeyer & Bruza, 2012):**
  - Quantum cognition suggests that human decision-making processes are not always linear or rational, but can instead follow probabilistic patterns similar to quantum mechanics. DEM can be integrated with quantum decision theory to create communication technologies that better reflect the complexity and unpredictability of human thought processes.
  - In AI systems, DEM could be used to develop more flexible and adaptive decision-making algorithms that account for the probabilistic nature of human cognition. This would enable AI to engage in more nuanced and context-sensitive interactions, improving its ability to understand and respond to users' needs.
- **Application of Quantum Decision Theory in AI (Pothos & Busemeyer, 2013):**
  - Quantum decision theory can inform the development of AI systems that are better equipped to handle uncertainty and ambiguity in human communication. DEM could be applied to these systems to enable them to dynamically adjust their communication strategies based on the probabilistic outcomes of user interactions.
  - For example, an AI-powered financial advisor could use

DEM to provide personalized investment recommendations that take into account the user's risk tolerance and decision-making style. By integrating quantum decision theory, the AI could adapt its recommendations based on the user's changing preferences and market conditions, offering more effective and responsive financial advice.

Phenomenological Control and Consciousness in VR/AR

The intersection of DEM with consciousness studies and phenomenological control offers exciting possibilities for enhancing communication technologies, particularly in VR/AR environments.

- **Phenomenological Control and Consciousness Studies (Grof, 2000; Wilber, 2006):**
  - Phenomenological control refers to the ability to influence one's subjective experiences, which can be harnessed to create more immersive and transformative communication experiences in VR/AR. DEM can be integrated with phenomenological control to enhance the user's sense of presence and engagement in virtual environments.
  - In VR/AR, DEM could be used to create experiences that adapt to the user's conscious state, offering tailored interactions that align with the user's psychological and emotional needs. For example, a VR-based therapy program could use DEM to guide the user's experience based on their emotional responses, providing personalized therapeutic interventions that promote healing and self-discovery.
- **Speculative Applications of DEM in Consciousness Studies:**
  - The integration of DEM with consciousness studies opens up possibilities for exploring the deeper dimensions of human experience through communication technologies. Future applications could include VR/AR environments that facilitate transpersonal experiences, where users

engage in deep, meaningful interactions that transcend ordinary reality.

- These speculative applications could be used in fields such as education, therapy, and spiritual practice, offering new ways to explore and expand human consciousness. DEM would play a key role in guiding these experiences, ensuring that they are both safe and transformative.

Scenarios and Case Studies: Future Applications of DEM

To illustrate the potential future applications of DEM in communication technologies, this section presents several scenarios and case studies that explore how DEM could be integrated into emerging technologies.

- **Scenario 1: DEM in an AI-Powered Virtual Classroom**:
    - **Context**: A virtual classroom uses AI and VR to create an immersive learning environment where students from around the world can engage in real-time interactions with instructors and peers.
    - **Application of DEM**: The AI system uses DEM to adapt its communication style based on the student's learning preferences and emotional state. During lectures, the system uses the Directive Mode to present key concepts clearly, while in discussion sessions, it switches to the Exploratory Mode to encourage student participation and critical thinking.
    - **Outcomes**: The DEM-enhanced virtual classroom leads to higher levels of student engagement and learning outcomes, as the AI adapts to meet the needs of each student. The use of DEM also fosters a more inclusive and supportive learning environment, where students feel empowered to explore new ideas and collaborate with their peers.
- **Case Study 1: DEM in a Healthcare AI System**:
    - **Context**: A healthcare provider implements an AI system

that uses VR to deliver personalized therapy sessions for patients with anxiety and depression.

- **Application of DEM**: The AI system uses DEM to tailor the therapy sessions to each patient's emotional state and therapeutic goals. The Directive Mode is used to guide the patient through relaxation exercises, while the Exploratory Mode encourages the patient to reflect on their experiences and emotions.
- **Outcomes**: The DEM-based AI system leads to significant improvements in patient outcomes, as the therapy sessions are personalized to address the specific needs of each patient. The use of DEM also enhances the therapeutic relationship, as patients feel more understood and supported by the AI system.

- **Case Study 2: DEM in a Corporate Communication Platform**:

  - **Context**: A multinational corporation develops a communication platform that uses AI and AR to facilitate collaboration among global teams.
  - **Application of DEM**: The platform uses DEM to adapt its communication strategies based on the cultural and linguistic backgrounds of the users. The Directive Mode is used to ensure clear and consistent messaging across all teams, while the Exploratory Mode fosters open dialogue and idea-sharing among team members.
  - **Outcomes**: The DEM-enhanced platform leads to improved communication and collaboration across the corporation's global teams. The use of DEM also helps to bridge cultural differences, creating a more cohesive and productive work environment.

Future Research Directions in DEM and Communication Technologies

As the integration of DEM into communication technologies continues to evolve, there are numerous opportunities for future research to explore its impact and potential.

- **Research on DEM in Emerging Communication Technologies**:
    - Future research could investigate the application of DEM in emerging communication technologies, such as AI, VR/AR, and neuromemristive systems. Studies could explore how DEM can enhance the adaptability, effectiveness, and ethical considerations of these technologies.
    - Comparative studies could also examine the effectiveness of DEM-based communication technologies compared to traditional approaches, providing insights into the unique benefits and challenges of using DEM in these contexts.
- **Development of DEM-Based Communication Tools**:
    - There is potential for the development of communication tools and platforms that integrate DEM into emerging technologies. These tools could include AI-powered communication systems, VR/AR environments, and neuromemristive systems that use DEM to create more personalized and adaptive interactions.
    - Research could focus on the development and validation of these tools, ensuring that they are effective in enhancing communication outcomes and addressing the ethical implications of their use.
- **Exploration of Consciousness Studies and DEM in Technology**:
    - As DEM is integrated into communication technologies, there is an opportunity to explore its potential impact on consciousness studies and phenomenological control. Future research could investigate how DEM can be used to create transformative experiences in VR/AR and other immersive technologies, offering new ways to explore and expand human consciousness.
    - Research could also explore the ethical implications of using DEM in these contexts, ensuring that the technology is used responsibly and that it promotes positive outcomes for users.

Conclusion

Chapter 19 has provided a comprehensive exploration of the potential impact of the Dual-Mode Elicitation Model (DEM) on the future of communication technologies. By integrating insights from future communication trends, VR/AR, neuromemristive systems, cybernetics, embodied cognition, quantum decision theory, and consciousness studies, this chapter has demonstrated the transformative potential of DEM in shaping the next generation of communication systems. The scenarios and case studies presented offer practical examples of how DEM could be applied to create more adaptive, personalized, and ethical communication technologies. As researchers and developers continue to explore the possibilities of DEM in these emerging fields, its application holds great promise for advancing human communication and expanding the frontiers of AI, consciousness, and transpersonal psychology.

21.

The Enduring Impact of DEM

Introduction

The Dual-Mode Elicitation Model (DEM) has been extensively explored throughout this manual, revealing its potential to revolutionize communication, education, healthcare, marketing, and AI technologies. As we conclude this comprehensive exploration, it is essential to reflect on the enduring impact of DEM and its transformative potential across various fields. This chapter synthesizes the research and applications discussed, considers the long-term implications of DEM in AI and human-machine interaction, and emphasizes the model's ability to adapt to new challenges and opportunities. By integrating cross-disciplinary insights, particularly from cybernetics and phenomenological control, we can better understand how DEM will continue to shape emerging technologies and interdisciplinary research.

The Transformative Potential of DEM

DEM stands out as a foundational model that offers a versatile framework for optimizing communication across diverse contexts. Its ability to balance directive and exploratory modes of communication makes it applicable to a wide range of fields, each of which benefits from DEM's capacity to adapt and enhance interactions.

- **Synthesis of Research and Applications**:
    - Throughout this manual, DEM has been shown to enhance communication strategies in various sectors. In education, DEM fosters more engaging and adaptive teaching methods that cater to individual learning styles (Sweller, 1988). In healthcare, DEM improves patient-centered care

by facilitating better understanding and empathy between providers and patients (LeDoux, 1996). In AI, DEM enables the development of systems that can simulate human communication more effectively, leading to advancements in human-machine interaction (Kandel, 2006).

- The synthesis of research across these fields demonstrates that DEM is not just a theoretical model but a practical tool with far-reaching applications. Its interdisciplinary nature allows it to integrate insights from cognitive psychology, neuroscience, communication theory, and other disciplines, making it a robust model capable of addressing complex communication challenges.

- **Long-Term Implications in AI and Human-Machine Interaction:**

  - One of the most significant areas where DEM's impact will be felt is in AI and human-machine interaction. As AI systems become more sophisticated, the ability to communicate effectively with humans becomes increasingly critical. DEM provides a framework for developing AI systems that can balance structured, directive communication with more open, exploratory dialogue, making these systems more intuitive and responsive to user needs (Gallagher, 2005).

  - The long-term implications of DEM in AI extend to various applications, including virtual assistants, customer service bots, and AI-driven educational tools. By enabling AI to communicate in ways that are more aligned with human cognitive processes, DEM contributes to the development of AI systems that are not only more effective but also more ethical and user-friendly.

Cross-Disciplinary Integration and the Evolution of DEM

One of the key strengths of DEM is its ability to integrate insights from multiple disciplines, creating a model that is both comprehensive and adaptable. This cross-disciplinary integration is crucial for the ongoing evolution of DEM and its ability to meet new challenges.

- **Linking Cybernetics and Phenomenological Control**:
  - The integration of cybernetics and phenomenological control within DEM offers a unique approach to understanding and optimizing communication. Cybernetics, with its emphasis on feedback loops and system regulation, provides a framework for understanding how communication systems can be designed to adapt and respond to changing conditions (Wiener, 1948). Phenomenological control, on the other hand, focuses on the subjective experience of communication, emphasizing the importance of context and interpretation (Carhart-Harris et al., 2014).
  - By linking these two perspectives, DEM offers a holistic approach to communication that considers both the objective and subjective aspects of interaction. This integration is particularly valuable in fields like VR/AR and AI, where understanding the user's experience is as important as ensuring the system's functionality.
- **Ongoing Evolution and Adaptation of DEM**:
  - As new technologies and communication challenges emerge, DEM must continue to evolve. The model's adaptability is one of its core strengths, allowing it to be applied in new contexts and with new technologies. For example, as quantum decision theory and embodied cognition gain traction in AI and communication research, DEM can be adapted to incorporate these insights, ensuring that it remains relevant and effective (Busemeyer & Bruza, 2012; Gallagher, 2005).
  - The ongoing evolution of DEM also involves refining its ethical considerations. As discussed in Chapter 17, the ethical implications of using DEM in AI, healthcare, and other fields must be carefully considered. The model must

continue to evolve to address these ethical challenges, ensuring that it is used in ways that promote fairness, transparency, and respect for autonomy (Dignum, 2018).

The Future of DEM in Emerging Technologies and Interdisciplinary Research

As we look to the future, DEM's role in emerging technologies and interdisciplinary research will be increasingly important. The model's ability to adapt and integrate new insights positions it as a key tool for advancing communication technologies and understanding complex human interactions.

- **Shaping Emerging Technologies**:
  - DEM's application in emerging technologies such as VR/AR, neuromemristive systems, and quantum cognition is likely to have a profound impact on how these technologies are developed and used. By providing a framework for adaptive and responsive communication, DEM can help ensure that these technologies are designed with the user's experience in mind, leading to more effective and satisfying interactions (Lanier, 2017; Mead, 2020).
  - The potential for DEM to influence AI and machine learning is particularly significant. As AI systems become more autonomous, the need for them to communicate effectively with humans becomes critical. DEM offers a model for creating AI that can adapt its communication strategies based on the user's needs and the context of the interaction, leading to more intuitive and human-like AI systems (Pothos & Busemeyer, 2013).
- **Expanding Interdisciplinary Research**:
  - The interdisciplinary nature of DEM makes it a valuable tool for research that spans multiple fields. As researchers continue to explore the intersections between communication, psychology, neuroscience, and AI, DEM

offers a model that can be used to integrate these diverse perspectives and generate new insights.

- Future research could explore the application of DEM in areas such as transpersonal psychology, where the model could be used to study how communication influences and is influenced by states of consciousness (Grof, 2000). Additionally, DEM could be applied to research in social robotics, where understanding the nuances of human communication is essential for developing robots that can interact effectively with people.

Final Thoughts and Future Directions

As we conclude this manual, it is clear that DEM holds significant potential for transforming communication across a wide range of fields. Its ability to adapt to new challenges and integrate cross-disciplinary insights makes it a foundational model for the future of communication, AI, and beyond.

- **A Forward-Looking Perspective:**
  - The future of DEM is bright, with opportunities for its application expanding as new technologies and research areas emerge. As we continue to explore the potential of DEM, it will be essential to remain open to new insights and innovations, ensuring that the model remains at the cutting edge of communication research and practice.
  - The continued refinement and evolution of DEM will require collaboration across disciplines, as well as a commitment to ethical considerations. By working together, researchers, practitioners, and developers can ensure that DEM is used to create communication systems that are not only effective but also ethical and respectful of human dignity.
- **The Enduring Impact of DEM:**
  - DEM's impact is likely to be enduring, influencing the way we think about and approach communication for

generations to come. As we continue to explore its potential, DEM will remain a vital tool for enhancing communication in education, healthcare, marketing, AI, and beyond.

- The enduring impact of DEM will also be seen in its ability to inspire new research and innovation. By providing a flexible and adaptable framework for communication, DEM will continue to shape the future of technology and interdisciplinary research, ensuring that communication remains a central focus in our rapidly changing world.

References

Cognitive Psychology and Neuroscience

- Bandura, A. (1986). *Social foundations of thought and action: A social cognitive theory.* Prentice-Hall.
- Damasio, A. R. (1994). *Descartes' error: Emotion, reason, and the human brain.* G.P. Putnam's Sons.
- Gallagher, S. (2005). *How the body shapes the mind.* Oxford University Press.
- Gazzaniga, M. S. (2011). *Who's in charge? Free will and the science of the brain.* HarperCollins.
- Kahneman, D. (2011). *Thinking, fast and slow.* Farrar, Straus and Giroux.
- Kandel, E. R. (2006). *In search of memory: The emergence of a new science of mind.* W. W. Norton & Company.
- LeDoux, J. E. (1996). *The emotional brain: The mysterious underpinnings of emotional life.* Simon & Schuster.
- Sweller, J. (1988). Cognitive load during problem solving: Effects on learning. *Cognitive Science, 12*(2), 257-285. https://doi.org/10.1207/s15516709cog1202_4

Communication Theory and General Semantics

- Hayakawa, S. I. (1949). *Language in thought and action.* Harcourt, Brace & World.
- Johnson, W. (1946). *People in quandaries: The semantics of personal adjustment.* Harper & Brothers.
- Korzybski, A. (1933). *Science and sanity: An introduction to non-Aristotelian systems and general semantics.* Institute of General

Semantics.

- McLuhan, M. (1964). *Understanding media: The extensions of man*. McGraw-Hill.

AI Development and Explainable AI (XAI)

- Busemeyer, J. R., & Bruza, P. D. (2012). *Quantum models of cognition and decision*. Cambridge University Press.
- Doshi-Velez, F., & Kim, B. (2017). Towards a rigorous science of interpretable machine learning. *arXiv preprint arXiv:1702.08608*.
- Gunning, D., Stefik, M., Choi, J., Miller, T., Stumpf, S., & Yang, G. Z. (2019). XAI—Explainable artificial intelligence. *Science Robotics*, 4(37), eaay7120. https://doi.org/10.1126/scirobotics.aay7120
- Mead, C. (1990). Neuromorphic electronic systems. *Proceedings of the IEEE*, 78(10), 1629-1636. https://doi.org/10.1109/5.58356
- Pinker, S. (1994). *The language instinct: How the mind creates language*. William Morrow and Company.

Behavioral Economics and Decision Theory

- Sunstein, C. R., & Thaler, R. H. (2008). *Nudge: Improving decisions about health, wealth, and happiness*. Yale University Press.
- Tversky, A., & Kahneman, D. (1974). Judgment under uncertainty: Heuristics and biases. *Science*, 185(4157), 1124-1131. https://doi.org/10.1126/science.185.4157.1124

Education and Instructional Design

- Bandura, A. (1977). *Social learning theory*. Prentice-Hall.
- Carhart-Harris, R. L., Leech, R., Hellyer, P. J., Shanahan, M., Feilding, A., Tagliazucchi, E., ... & Nutt, D. (2014). The entropic brain: A theory of conscious states informed by neuroimaging

research with psychedelic drugs. *Frontiers in Human Neuroscience, 8*, 20. https://doi.org/10.3389/fnhum.2014.00020

- Dewey, J. (1938). *Experience and education.* Macmillan.
- Sweller, J. (2010). *Cognitive load theory: Recent theoretical advances.* Springer.

Ethics and Bioethics

- Dignum, V. (2018). *Responsible artificial intelligence: Designing AI for human values.* Springer Nature.
- Lin, P. (2016). Why ethics matters for autonomous cars. In *Autonomes fahren* (pp. 69-85). Springer Vieweg, Berlin, Heidelberg. https://doi.org/10.1007/978-3-662-48847-8_5
- Kant, I. (1785). *Groundwork for the metaphysics of morals* (M. Gregor, Trans.). Cambridge University Press. (Original work published 1785)

Signature-Based AI and Psychometrics

- Kosinski, M., Stillwell, D., & Graepel, T. (2013). Private traits and attributes are predictable from digital records of human behavior. *Proceedings of the National Academy of Sciences, 110*(15), 5802-5805. https://doi.org/10.1073/pnas.1218772110
- Pinker, S. (1997). *How the mind works.* Norton.
- Sutton, R. S., & Barto, A. G. (2018). *Reinforcement learning: An introduction* (2nd ed.). MIT Press.

Miscellaneous and Interdisciplinary

- Beer, S. (1972). *Brain of the firm: The managerial cybernetics of organization.* Herder and Herder.
- Foerster, H. von. (2003). *Understanding understanding: Essays on cybernetics and cognition.* Springer-Verlag.
- Wiener, N. (1950). *The human use of human beings: Cybernetics*

and society. Houghton Mifflin.

Appendix A: Glossary of Terms and Concepts

This glossary provides clear, concise definitions and explanations of key terms and concepts used throughout the manual. These definitions are drawn from and integrated with concepts from cognitive psychology, neuroscience, cybernetics, communication theory, phenomenological control, and consciousness studies. This resource is intended to aid readers in understanding the interdisciplinary nature of the Dual-Mode Elicitation Model (DEM) and its application across various fields.

Adaptive Communication Systems

Definition: Systems designed to adjust their communication strategies in real-time based on feedback from the environment or users.

Context: In DEM, adaptive communication systems utilize both directive and exploratory modes to optimize interaction outcomes. This concept is rooted in cybernetic principles where feedback loops are essential for continuous adaptation and improvement (Wiener, 1948).

Artificial Emotional Intelligence (AEI)

Definition: A subfield of AI focused on the development of systems that can recognize, interpret, and respond to human emotions.

Context: AEI is relevant to DEM as it enables AI systems to engage in more empathetic communication, enhancing their ability to respond to users in emotionally appropriate ways (Zeng et al., 2009).

Behavioral Economics

Definition: A field of study that examines the psychological, social, and emotional factors that influence economic decision-making.

Context: DEM integrates insights from behavioral economics to understand and influence decision-making processes in communication, particularly in marketing and sales contexts (Thaler & Sunstein, 2008).

Cognitive Load Theory (CLT)

Definition: A theory that explains the limitations of working memory and how excessive cognitive load can hinder learning and information processing.

Context: In DEM, CLT informs the balance between directive and exploratory communication, ensuring that messages are structured to optimize understanding without overwhelming the audience (Sweller, 1988).

Cybernetics

Definition: The study of systems, particularly the communication and control mechanisms within them, and their application in machines and living organisms.

Context: Cybernetics is foundational to DEM, particularly in the development of adaptive communication systems that respond to feedback and regulate their behavior to achieve desired outcomes (Wiener, 1948).

Directive Mode

Definition: A communication mode characterized by structured, goal-oriented interaction, focusing on clarity, precision, and efficiency.

Context: In DEM, the Directive Mode is employed when clear, direct communication is necessary to achieve specific outcomes, often in instructional or informational contexts (Kahneman, 2011).

Dual-Mode Elicitation Model (DEM)

Definition: A communication framework that optimizes interaction by dynamically integrating two modes—Directive and Exploratory—based on the needs of the context and participants.

Context: DEM is a versatile model applicable across various fields, including AI, education, healthcare, and strategic communication, facilitating effective and adaptive communication strategies.

Embodied Cognition

Definition: A theory that emphasizes the role of the body and its interactions with the environment in shaping the mind and cognitive processes.

Context: DEM leverages the principles of embodied cognition to enhance the naturalness and intuitiveness of communication, particularly in AI and VR/AR environments (Gallagher, 2005).

Explainable AI (XAI)

Definition: AI systems that are designed to provide clear, understandable explanations for their decisions and actions.

Context: DEM is integrated into XAI to ensure that communication with users is transparent and that the AI's reasoning processes are accessible, fostering trust and user engagement (Gunning, 2017).

Exploratory Mode

Definition: A communication mode characterized by open-ended, flexible interaction, encouraging creativity, discovery, and adaptability.

Context: In DEM, the Exploratory Mode is used in contexts where innovation, problem-solving, and deeper understanding are required, allowing for a more fluid and interactive communication process (Kahneman, 2011).

General Semantics

Definition: A field of study that examines how language and symbols influence human thought and behavior.

Context: General Semantics underpins the language strategies within DEM, emphasizing the role of language in shaping reality and guiding communication (Korzybski, 1933).

Human-Computer Interaction (HCI)

Definition: The study of how people interact with computers and other digital devices, focusing on improving the usability and user experience of these systems.

Context: DEM is applied in HCI to enhance the naturalness and effectiveness of interactions between humans and AI, making communication more intuitive and responsive (Shneiderman, 2010).

Neural Plasticity

Definition: The brain's ability to reorganize itself by forming new neural connections in response to learning, experience, or injury.

Context: DEM incorporates the concept of neural plasticity to understand how communication strategies can be adapted and optimized over time, particularly in educational and therapeutic contexts (Kandel, 2006).

Neuroscience of Emotion Regulation

Definition: The study of how the brain processes and regulates emotions, focusing on the neural mechanisms underlying emotional responses.

Context: DEM leverages insights from the neuroscience of emotion regulation to inform how communication strategies can be tailored to manage and respond to emotional states effectively (LeDoux, 1996).

Phenomenological Control

Definition: The ability to influence one's subjective experiences, particularly in contexts involving altered states of consciousness or immersive environments.

Context: In DEM, phenomenological control is used to enhance the user experience in VR/AR settings, allowing for more personalized and impactful interactions (Carhart-Harris et al., 2014).

Quantum Cognition

Definition: A theoretical approach that applies principles of quantum mechanics to understand cognitive processes, particularly decision-making and perception.

Context: DEM integrates quantum cognition to develop more sophisticated communication systems that can handle the complexity and uncertainty inherent in human thought processes (Busemeyer & Bruza, 2012).

Social Identity Theory

Definition: A theory that explores how individuals' sense of self is influenced by their membership in social groups and how this affects their behavior and attitudes.

Context: DEM incorporates Social Identity Theory to tailor communication strategies that resonate with the audience's social identities, enhancing engagement and relevance (Tajfel & Turner, 1979).

Virtual Reality (VR) and Augmented Reality (AR)

Definition: VR refers to immersive digital environments that simulate physical presence, while AR overlays digital information onto the physical world.

Context: DEM is applied in VR/AR to create more adaptive and interactive communication experiences, enhancing the realism and emotional impact of virtual interactions (Lanier, 2017).

Appendix B: Technical Appendices

Introduction

This appendix provides supplementary technical resources to support the practical implementation of the Dual Mode Elicitation Model (DEM) across various fields, including AI development, education, therapy, and strategic communication. The resources included are designed to offer professionals practical tools, templates, and methodologies for effectively applying DEM in their work. This section focuses on the intersection of cybernetics, AI ethics, and phenomenological control, integrating both technical aspects and practical applications.

B.1 Sample Algorithms for DEM Implementation

To facilitate the practical application of DEM in AI systems and other technology-driven contexts, this section provides sample algorithms that can be adapted for various use cases. These algorithms are designed to balance directive and exploratory modes of communication, allowing for dynamic interaction based on real-time feedback and user inputs.

B.1.1 Algorithm for Adaptive AI Chatbots

```python
python
Copy code
def dem_response(user_input, context):
    """

Determines the AI response mode (directive or exploratory) based on user input and context.

    """

    directive_keywords = ['how', 'what', 'when', 'where', 'why']
    exploratory_indicators = ['unsure', 'explore', 'discuss', 'think', 'maybe']
```

```python
    # Directive mode response
    if any(keyword in user_input.lower() for keyword in
directive_keywords):
        response_mode = "directive"
        response = generate_directive_response(user_input, context)

    # Exploratory mode response
    elif any(indicator in user_input.lower() for indicator in
exploratory_indicators):
        response_mode = "exploratory"
        response = generate_exploratory_response(user_input, context)

    # Default to directive if no indicators found
    else:
        response_mode = "directive"
        response = generate_directive_response(user_input, context)

    return response_mode, response

def generate_directive_response(user_input, context):
    # Implement logic for directive mode response
    response = f"Here is a clear answer to your question about
{context}."
    return response

def generate_exploratory_response(user_input, context):
    # Implement logic for exploratory mode response
    response = f"Let's explore this further. What are your thoughts on
{context}?"
    return response

# Example usage
user_input = "Can you explain how this works?"
context = "AI ethics"
mode, response = dem_response(user_input, context)
```

```python
print(f"Mode: {mode}, Response: {response}")
```

Explanation:

This algorithm dynamically determines whether the AI should respond in a directive or exploratory mode based on the user's input. It allows the AI to switch between providing clear, direct answers and engaging in more open-ended discussions, enhancing the interaction's effectiveness and adaptability.

B.1.2 Algorithm for Educational Adaptive Learning Systems

```python
python
Copy code
def adaptive_learning_module(student_responses, learning_objectives):
    """
    Adapts the learning module content based on student responses
    and learning objectives.
    """

    progress = assess_student_progress(student_responses)

    if progress < 0.5:
        mode = "directive"
        module_content = provide_directive_instruction(learning_objectives)
    else:
        mode = "exploratory"
        module_content = provide_exploratory_learning(learning_objectives)

    return mode, module_content

def assess_student_progress(responses):
    # Logic to assess student progress
    progress_score = sum(responses) / len(responses)
    return progress_score

def provide_directive_instruction(objectives):
```

```python
    # Logic to provide directive instruction
    content = f"Focusing on key concepts: {objectives}. Here's what you need to know."
    return content


def provide_exploratory_learning(objectives):
    # Logic to encourage exploratory learning
    content = f"Let's dive deeper into these topics: {objectives}. What interests you the most?"
    return content


# Example usage
student_responses = [0.6, 0.4, 0.7, 0.5]
learning_objectives = "Cybernetics and AI Ethics"
mode, content = adaptive_learning_module(student_responses, learning_objectives)
print(f"Mode: {mode}, Content: {content}")
```

Explanation:

This adaptive learning algorithm adjusts the content of an educational module based on the student's progress. By switching between directive instruction and exploratory learning, it ensures that students receive the support they need to achieve learning objectives while also encouraging deeper exploration of topics they find engaging.

B.2 Code Snippets for DEM Integration in Communication Platforms

This section provides code snippets that demonstrate how DEM can be integrated into various communication platforms, such as customer service systems, virtual learning environments, and therapeutic applications.

B.2.1 Integrating DEM in Customer Service Platforms

python

Copy code

```python
class CustomerServiceAI:
```

```python
    def __init__(self):
    self.history = []

    def handle_query(self, query):
    mode = self.determine_mode(query)
    if mode == "directive":
    response = self.directive_response(query)
    else:
    response = self.exploratory_response(query)
    self.history.append((query, response))
    return response

    def determine_mode(self, query):
    if "return" in query or "refund" in query:
    return "directive"
    else:
    return "exploratory"

    def directive_response(self, query):
    return "I can help you with your return. Please provide your order
number."

    def exploratory_response(self, query):
    return "It seems you're looking for advice. What products are you
interested in?"

    # Example usage
    cs_ai = CustomerServiceAI()
    query = "I'm not sure which product to choose."
    response = cs_ai.handle_query(query)
    print(response)
```

Explanation:

This snippet demonstrates how a customer service AI might use
DEM to determine whether to provide a directive response (e.g.,
handling a return) or an exploratory response (e.g., helping a

customer choose a product). This approach ensures that the AI can handle both straightforward queries and more complex, nuanced interactions.

B.3 Case Studies: Practical Applications of DEM

B.3.1 Case Study: Applying DEM in Virtual Therapy

Context:

A mental health provider uses a virtual reality (VR) platform to conduct therapy sessions for patients with anxiety. The platform integrates DEM to adapt the therapy based on the patient's real-time emotional responses.

Implementation:

- **Directive Mode**: The therapist uses directive communication to guide patients through relaxation exercises, providing clear instructions to ensure effectiveness.
- **Exploratory Mode**: When patients express uncertainty or emotional distress, the platform switches to exploratory communication, encouraging them to share their feelings and thoughts in a safe, supportive environment.

Outcome:

Patients report a significant reduction in anxiety symptoms and an increased sense of control over their emotions. The use of DEM enables the therapy to be both structured and responsive to the patient's needs.

B.3.2 Case Study: DEM in Strategic Communication Campaigns

Context:

A nonprofit organization uses DEM to design a public awareness campaign about climate change. The campaign targets diverse demographic groups, each with different levels of knowledge and concern about the issue.

Implementation:

- **Directive Mode**: For audiences less familiar with climate change, the campaign uses directive messaging to provide clear, factual information about the issue and its impacts.

- **Exploratory Mode**: For more engaged audiences, the campaign encourages dialogue and exploration of solutions, fostering a deeper connection with the cause.

Outcome:

The campaign achieves widespread awareness and engagement, with significant increases in public knowledge and activism. By tailoring the communication strategy to the audience's level of engagement, DEM helps the organization reach a broad and diverse audience effectively.

B.4 Technical Documentation and Implementation Guides

This section provides documentation and guides for implementing DEM in various professional contexts, offering step-by-step instructions, best practices, and troubleshooting tips.

B.4.1 Implementing DEM in AI Systems: A Step-by-Step Guide

- **Step 1**: Define the communication objectives for the AI system, identifying scenarios where directive and exploratory modes will be applied.
- **Step 2**: Develop algorithms that allow the AI to switch between modes based on user input and contextual factors.
- **Step 3**: Integrate the algorithms into the AI system, ensuring compatibility with existing software architecture.
- **Step 4**: Test the system in real-world scenarios, gathering feedback to refine and improve the DEM implementation.
- **Step 5**: Monitor the system's performance over time, making adjustments as needed to maintain optimal communication outcomes.

B.4.2 Best Practices for Using DEM in Educational Technology

- **Design for Flexibility**: Ensure that the educational platform can adapt its communication strategies based on student progress and feedback.

- **Balance Structure and Exploration**: Use directive communication to introduce key concepts clearly, while allowing exploratory communication to foster deeper engagement and critical thinking.
- **Incorporate Feedback Mechanisms**: Continuously gather and analyze student feedback to refine the use of DEM and improve learning outcomes.

B.4.3 Troubleshooting Common Issues in DEM Integration

- **Issue 1**: The AI system frequently misidentifies the appropriate communication mode.
  - **Solution**: Refine the mode-determination algorithm by incorporating additional contextual indicators and user feedback.
- **Issue 2**: Users find the communication too rigid or too ambiguous.
  - **Solution**: Adjust the balance between directive and exploratory modes, providing clearer guidelines or more opportunities for open-ended interaction as needed.
- **Issue 3**: The system struggles to handle complex, nuanced interactions.
  - **Solution**: Enhance the AI's natural language processing capabilities and ensure that the system has access to a robust knowledge base for handling diverse queries.

Conclusion

Appendix B provides technical resources, algorithms, code snippets, case studies, and implementation guides to help professionals apply the Dual Mode Elicitation Model (DEM) effectively across various fields. These tools are designed to support the integration of DEM into AI systems, educational platforms, therapeutic environments, and strategic communication campaigns. By offering practical guidance and technical documentation, this appendix ensures that readers have the resources they need to implement DEM successfully and achieve optimal communication outcomes.

Case Studies: The Directive Mode in Action

2.5 Case Studies: The Directive Mode in Action

This section presents detailed scenarios and step-by-step walkthroughs for the application of the Directive Mode in various fields. Each case study is designed to help readers understand how to effectively implement the Directive Mode within the context of AI-powered customer service systems, Cognitive-Behavioral Therapy (CBT) interventions, and strategic health communication campaigns.

Case Study 1: AI-Powered Customer Service Systems

Scenario:

An e-commerce company has developed an AI-powered customer service system to handle common customer inquiries, such as order status, returns, and product information. The goal is to provide clear, concise responses that guide users toward resolving their issues efficiently without the need for human intervention.

Step-by-Step Walkthrough:

1. **Understanding the User's Query:**

   - The AI system first processes the customer's inquiry using natural language processing (NLP). For example, if a customer types, "Where is my order?" the system recognizes this as a request for order status.
   - The system categorizes the query under a predefined set of directives, such as "Order Status," "Returns," or "Product Information."

2. **Selecting the Directive Mode:**

- Given the straightforward nature of the inquiry, the system selects the Directive Mode to provide a clear and concise response. The aim is to deliver the necessary information directly, minimizing the need for further clarification.

3. **Generating the Response:**

   - The AI retrieves the relevant data, such as tracking information, and formulates a response. For instance, "Your order is currently in transit and is expected to arrive by [specific date]. You can track it here: [tracking link]."
   - The response is structured to be easily understood, with no extraneous information that could confuse the customer.

4. **Handling Potential Follow-Up Questions:**

   - The system anticipates common follow-up questions (e.g., "What if my order doesn't arrive on time?") and prepares additional directive responses. For example, "If your order does not arrive by [specific date], please contact us, and we will assist you further."
   - This step ensures that the user feels guided through the process without ambiguity or the need for multiple interactions.

5. **Feedback and Adjustment:**

   - The AI system tracks user satisfaction through quick surveys or by analyzing whether users ask for additional help after receiving a response. If many users ask for further clarification, the system updates its response strategies to improve clarity.

Embedded Example:

Customer Query: "How do I return a product?"

- AI Response: "To return a product, please follow these steps: 1) Log into your account, 2) Go to 'Order History,' 3) Select the item you want to return, 4) Click on 'Request Return,' 5) Print the return label and ship the item back to us. For more detailed instructions, visit [return policy link]."

Outcome:

By using the Directive Mode, the AI system efficiently resolves customer inquiries, reducing the need for human intervention and increasing customer satisfaction. The clear and concise responses help customers quickly understand the steps they need to take, leading to a smoother user experience.

Case Study 2: Cognitive-Behavioral Therapy (CBT) Interventions
   Scenario:

A therapist is working with a patient diagnosed with anxiety. The therapist uses Cognitive-Behavioral Therapy (CBT), a structured, directive form of psychotherapy that helps patients identify and change negative thought patterns and behaviors. The goal is to guide the patient through specific coping strategies that can be applied in moments of high anxiety.

   Step-by-Step Walkthrough:

1. **Identifying the Problem:**

   - The therapist begins the session by asking the patient to describe a recent situation where they felt anxious. The patient might say, "I felt really anxious before a meeting at work because I thought I would mess up."
   - The therapist identifies the underlying cognitive distortion, such as "catastrophizing" (expecting the worst possible outcome).

2. **Directive Mode Intervention:**

- The therapist then shifts to the Directive Mode to guide the patient in restructuring this thought. The therapist might say, "Let's take that thought and challenge it. What's the evidence that you will mess up in the meeting? And what's the evidence against it?"
- The therapist directs the patient to consider both sides, helping them see that their fear might be exaggerated.

3. **Teaching Coping Strategies**:

- The therapist introduces a specific coping strategy, such as "thought stopping" or "reframing." For instance, the therapist might say, "Next time you have this thought, try saying 'Stop!' in your mind, and then replace it with a more balanced thought, like 'I've prepared for this meeting, and I can handle it.'"
- The therapist practices this with the patient, ensuring they understand how to apply the technique in real-life situations.

4. **Homework Assignment**:

- The therapist assigns homework to reinforce the directive intervention. For example, "This week, I want you to practice this technique whenever you feel anxious before a meeting. Write down the original thought, how you challenged it, and the new thought you replaced it with."
- This structured approach helps the patient apply the skills learned in therapy to their daily life.

5. **Review and Reinforcement**:

- In the following session, the therapist reviews the homework with the patient, providing positive reinforcement for their efforts and offering further guidance if needed. The therapist might say, "You did a great job identifying your thoughts and challenging them. Let's build on that by applying this technique to other areas where you feel anxious."

Embedded Example:

Patient Statement: "I'm going to fail this presentation, and everyone will think I'm incompetent."

- Therapist Directive: "Let's break that down. What's the evidence that you will fail? And what's the evidence that you might succeed? Once we challenge this thought, what would be a more balanced way of thinking about the presentation?"

Outcome:

The Directive Mode in CBT provides the patient with clear, structured steps to manage their anxiety. By focusing on specific cognitive distortions and teaching coping strategies, the therapist helps the patient develop the tools they need to handle anxiety-provoking situations more effectively.

Case Study 3: Strategic Health Communication Campaigns

Scenario:

A public health organization is launching a campaign to increase vaccination rates in a community with low uptake. The campaign uses the Directive Mode to deliver clear, goal-oriented messaging designed to overcome hesitancy and encourage action.

Step-by-Step Walkthrough:

1. **Defining the Target Audience**:

   ◦ The organization identifies key demographics within the community that are less likely to get vaccinated, such as young adults and individuals with specific cultural or religious concerns.

2. **Crafting Directive Messages**:

- The messaging is developed to address common concerns directly and encourage vaccination. For example, "Vaccination is safe and effective. Protect yourself and your loved ones—get vaccinated today at your nearest clinic."
- Messages are concise, focusing on the benefits of vaccination and the risks of remaining unvaccinated. Each message includes a clear call to action, such as "Call [hotline number] or visit [website] to book your appointment."

3. **Selecting Communication Channels**:

- The campaign utilizes various channels to disseminate these messages, including social media, radio ads, and community posters. The directive nature of the messaging ensures that the information is easily understood and can be acted upon immediately.
- For instance, social media posts might feature testimonials from trusted community leaders with a simple, directive message: "I got vaccinated to protect my family. You can too—get your shot today."

4. **Addressing Misinformation**:

- Part of the directive messaging strategy includes directly addressing and correcting misinformation. For example, "Contrary to some myths, vaccines do not cause infertility. They protect you from serious illness. Get the facts—talk to your doctor."
- The campaign provides links to official resources and encourages individuals to seek information from credible sources.

5. **Measuring Impact and Adjusting Strategy**:

- The organization monitors vaccination rates and public feedback to assess the campaign's effectiveness. If certain messages are not resonating, they refine the directive content to better address community concerns.
- For example, if data shows that younger adults are still hesitant, the organization might adjust its strategy to include more peer-driven messages, such as "Join your friends in getting vaccinated—let's protect our community together."

Embedded Example:

Campaign Message: "Vaccines save lives. Protect yourself from COVID-19—get vaccinated today at [location]. It's quick, safe, and free. For more information, visit [website] or call [hotline]."

Outcome:

The Directive Mode in the health communication campaign leads to a measurable increase in vaccination rates. The clear, goal-oriented messaging effectively addresses community concerns and provides straightforward instructions on how to get vaccinated, making it easier for individuals to take action.

Conclusion

These case studies illustrate how the Directive Mode of the Dual Mode Elicitation Model (DEM) can be effectively applied across different fields. By providing step-by-step walkthroughs and embedded examples, this section offers practical guidance on implementing directive communication strategies to achieve specific outcomes, whether in AI-powered customer service, Cognitive-Behavioral Therapy, or public health campaigns. Through these examples, readers can better understand the "how to" of DEM and apply its principles in their professional contexts.

Case Studies: The Exploratory Mode in Action

3.5 Case Studies: The Exploratory Mode in Action

This section presents detailed scenarios and step-by-step walkthroughs to demonstrate the application of the Exploratory Mode in various fields, including project-based learning in education, narrative therapy in mental health, and AI in creative industries. These case studies are designed to help readers understand the practical implementation of the Exploratory Mode in the Dual Mode Elicitation Model (DEM), showcasing how open-ended communication fosters creativity, critical thinking, and innovation.

Case Study 1: Project-Based Learning in Education

Scenario:

A high school science teacher is implementing a project-based learning (PBL) approach in their classroom. The goal is to encourage students to explore real-world environmental problems and develop innovative solutions. The teacher uses the Exploratory Mode to guide students through the process, fostering critical thinking, collaboration, and creativity.

Step-by-Step Walkthrough:

1. **Introduction to the Project:**

   - The teacher introduces the project by presenting a broad, open-ended problem: "Our city is facing increasing levels of air pollution. How can we reduce air pollution in our community?"
   - Instead of providing specific instructions, the teacher encourages students to brainstorm possible causes and solutions. This sets the stage for exploratory learning,

where students take the lead in their own inquiry.

2. **Facilitating Group Discussions**:

    ◦ The teacher divides the class into small groups, each
      tasked with exploring different aspects of the problem. For
      example, one group might investigate the sources of
      pollution, while another explores the impact on public
      health.
    ◦ During group discussions, the teacher uses open-ended
      questions to guide exploration: "What do you think are the
      main sources of air pollution in our city? How might
      different solutions impact these sources?"
    ◦ The teacher refrains from providing direct answers,
      instead encouraging students to consider various
      perspectives and potential solutions.

3. **Research and Exploration**:

    ◦ Students conduct research using various resources, such
      as scientific articles, interviews with local experts, and
      data collection. The teacher provides guidance on how to
      conduct research but allows students to decide which
      sources to use and how to analyze the information.
    ◦ The teacher remains available to support students but
      continues to use the Exploratory Mode: "How might this
      data change your understanding of the problem? What
      other factors should you consider as you develop your
      solution?"

4. **Developing and Presenting Solutions**:

    ◦ Each group develops a proposed solution to the pollution
      problem, which they will present to the class. The teacher
      encourages them to be creative and consider
      unconventional approaches: "What new ideas can you

bring to the table that haven't been tried before? How can your solution be both innovative and practical?"

- ○ The presentation phase is also exploratory. Students present their ideas and receive feedback from their peers and the teacher, who asks probing questions to encourage further reflection and refinement.

5. **Reflection and Iteration**:

- ○ After the presentations, the class engages in a reflective discussion on what they learned from the project and how their thinking evolved. The teacher uses the Exploratory Mode to guide this reflection: "How did your understanding of the problem change as you worked on this project? What would you do differently if you were to tackle a similar problem in the future?"
- ○ Students are encouraged to iterate on their solutions, incorporating feedback and new insights gained during the reflection.

Embedded Example:

Teacher Question: "What if the solution isn't just about reducing emissions? What if we also focused on increasing green spaces in the city? How could that impact air quality and public health?"

Outcome:

The Exploratory Mode in this project-based learning scenario fosters a deep engagement with the problem, encouraging students to think critically, collaborate effectively, and develop creative solutions. By guiding rather than directing, the teacher helps students take ownership of their learning and develop skills that are crucial for problem-solving in real-world contexts.

Case Study 2: Narrative Therapy in Mental Health

Scenario:

A therapist is working with a patient who has experienced trauma. The therapist uses narrative therapy, which emphasizes the

Exploratory Mode, to help the patient re-author their life story in a way that promotes healing and empowerment. The goal is to explore the patient's experiences and facilitate self-discovery and personal growth.

Step-by-Step Walkthrough:

1. **Creating a Safe Space for Exploration**:

   - The therapist begins by establishing a safe, non-judgmental space where the patient feels comfortable sharing their story. The therapist might say, "This is your time to share your story in your own way. We'll explore it together at your pace."
   - The therapist encourages the patient to speak freely, without guiding the conversation in a specific direction.

2. **Exploring the Patient's Narrative**:

   - As the patient begins to tell their story, the therapist listens actively, using the Exploratory Mode to ask open-ended questions: "What stands out to you the most when you think about that experience? How did it shape the person you are today?"
   - The therapist avoids making interpretations or judgments, allowing the patient to explore their narrative fully and identify significant themes on their own.

3. **Identifying Alternative Narratives**:

   - The therapist introduces the concept of alternative narratives, inviting the patient to consider different ways of viewing their experiences: "What if we looked at this part of your story from another angle? How might that change your understanding of what happened?"
   - The therapist encourages the patient to explore new perspectives and possibilities, helping them to see their

story in a more empowering light.

4. **Facilitating Self-Discovery and Re-Authoring**:

   - As the patient explores these alternative narratives, the therapist guides them in re-authoring their story. This process is exploratory and collaborative: "If you were to write a new chapter in your life story, what would you want it to be about? How would you describe yourself in this new narrative?"
   - The therapist helps the patient to identify strengths, resources, and new identities that emerge from this re-authoring process.

5. **Reflecting on the Process**:

   - The therapist encourages the patient to reflect on the changes in their narrative and how these changes affect their sense of self: "How does this new narrative feel different from the one you started with? What have you learned about yourself through this process?"
   - The reflection helps the patient internalize the growth and self-discovery achieved through the therapy.

Embedded Example:

Therapist Question: "If we think about this experience as a chapter in your life, what title would you give it? And what title would you want for the next chapter?"

Outcome:

The Exploratory Mode in narrative therapy allows the patient to explore their life story in a way that promotes healing and personal growth. By guiding the patient through an open-ended exploration of their narrative, the therapist helps them to re-author their story, leading to transformative therapeutic outcomes.

Case Study 3: AI in Creative Industries

Scenario:

A design firm uses an AI system to assist in generating novel concepts for branding projects. The AI is programmed to operate in the Exploratory Mode, helping human designers explore new artistic possibilities and push creative boundaries. The goal is to use the AI as a creative partner that suggests unconventional ideas and inspires innovation.

Step-by-Step Walkthrough:

1. **Initiating the Creative Process**:

   ◦ The design team begins by inputting basic project parameters into the AI system, such as the industry, target audience, and desired brand image. The AI uses this information to start generating a wide range of design concepts.

   ◦ The Exploratory Mode is activated, encouraging the AI to produce a variety of unconventional ideas that might not typically be considered in a standard design process.

2. **Generating and Exploring Concepts**:

   ◦ The AI presents several initial concepts to the design team, each with different visual styles, color schemes, and thematic elements. Instead of filtering out ideas that don't fit the norm, the AI includes a mix of traditional and avant-garde suggestions.

   ◦ The designers engage with the AI, exploring these concepts in depth: "What if we combined the modern minimalist style with the vintage typography you suggested? How would that change the brand's visual identity?"

3. **Iterative Exploration and Feedback**:

   ◦ The design team provides feedback on the concepts, and

the AI adjusts its suggestions accordingly. For example, if the team prefers a concept with bold colors but wants to see variations in layout, the AI generates new options that explore these aspects.

- The AI continues to operate in the Exploratory Mode, encouraging the team to consider various combinations and refinements: "Here are three new layouts based on your feedback. How might these different structures influence the brand's message?"

4. **Incorporating Human Creativity**:

- The designers use the AI-generated concepts as inspiration, blending their creative intuition with the AI's suggestions. This collaborative process helps the team push creative boundaries and explore ideas they might not have considered on their own.
- The Exploratory Mode ensures that the AI remains a source of inspiration rather than dictating the final design, allowing human creativity to guide the final product.

5. **Finalizing the Design**:

- After several rounds of exploration and iteration, the design team selects the final concept, incorporating both the AI's innovative suggestions and their own creative input.
- The team reflects on the collaborative process, considering how the AI's exploratory approach helped them achieve a more innovative and impactful design.

Embedded Example:
AI Suggestion: "What if we used a monochrome color palette with an abstract geometric pattern for the logo? This could give

the brand a modern, sophisticated look while standing out in the market."

Outcome:

The Exploratory Mode in AI-assisted design enables the creative team to explore a wide range of possibilities, leading to innovative and unique outcomes. By acting as a creative partner, the AI helps the designers push beyond conventional limits, resulting in a final product that is both distinctive and aligned with the client's vision.

Conclusion

These case studies illustrate how the Exploratory Mode of the Dual Mode Elicitation Model (DEM) can be effectively applied in various fields. Through detailed scenarios and step-by-step walkthroughs, this section demonstrates how open-ended communication fosters creativity, critical thinking, and innovation. Whether in education, therapy, or creative industries, the Exploratory Mode allows individuals and teams to explore new possibilities, leading to deeper understanding and more impactful outcomes.

Case Studies: Dynamic Integration in Practice

4.5 Case Studies: Dynamic Integration in Practice

This section provides detailed scenarios and step-by-step walkthroughs to demonstrate how dynamic integration, as outlined in the Dual Mode Elicitation Model (DEM), can be effectively applied across different fields. These case studies include applications in blended learning, integrative therapy, and adaptive AI systems in customer service. Each case study illustrates how the seamless integration of directive and exploratory modes enhances outcomes by leveraging the strengths of both approaches.

Case Study 1: Blended Learning in Education

   Scenario:

A high school history teacher is implementing a blended learning model in their classroom. The model combines online instruction, which uses the Directive Mode for delivering content, with in-class activities that utilize the Exploratory Mode to encourage deeper understanding and critical thinking. The goal is to create a seamless learning experience that maximizes student engagement and knowledge retention.

   Step-by-Step Walkthrough:

1. **Online Instruction (Directive Mode)**:

   - The teacher begins by assigning an online module on the causes of World War I. The module includes structured video lectures, readings, and quizzes that deliver key facts and concepts.
   - The online content is designed to be clear and concise, focusing on the essential information students need to understand the topic. The quizzes assess comprehension,

ensuring that students grasp the foundational knowledge before moving on.

2. **Transition to In-Class Exploration (Exploratory Mode)**:

   - After completing the online module, students come to class prepared to engage in exploratory activities. The teacher starts the class with an open-ended question: "What do you think were the most significant causes of World War I, and how might different perspectives influence our understanding of these causes?"
   - Students are divided into groups to discuss various perspectives, such as political, economic, and social factors. The teacher circulates the room, facilitating discussions by asking probing questions: "How might these causes be interconnected? What if one of these factors had been different—how could that have changed the course of history?"

3. **Dynamic Integration During Group Work**:

   - As groups discuss, the teacher dynamically shifts between directive and exploratory modes based on the needs of the students. For instance, if a group struggles with understanding a key concept from the online module, the teacher provides a brief, directive explanation to clarify the issue.
   - Conversely, when a group is deeply engaged in exploring a complex question, the teacher encourages them to continue exploring different viewpoints, using the Exploratory Mode to deepen their analysis.

4. **Class Discussion and Synthesis**:

   - After group discussions, the class comes together for a full-group discussion. The teacher uses a blend of directive and exploratory approaches to guide the synthesis of ideas: "Let's summarize the key causes you've identified. How do they fit together, and what new questions have emerged from your discussions?"

  ◦ The teacher integrates the group findings, helping students see the broader picture while also encouraging them to think critically about unresolved questions or alternative interpretations.

5. **Reflection and Application**:

  ◦ To conclude, the teacher assigns a reflective essay where students must use both the facts learned during the online module (Directive Mode) and the insights gained from in-class discussions (Exploratory Mode). The essay prompt might be: "Discuss the causes of World War I, incorporating both the factual information and the different perspectives explored in class. How does integrating these approaches change your understanding of the event?"

Embedded Example:

Teacher Directive: "Remember that the assassination of Archduke Franz Ferdinand was the immediate cause, but think about how underlying factors like alliances and nationalism played a role. How can we explore these connections further?"

Outcome:

Dynamic integration in the blended learning environment leads to a deeper understanding of historical events. Students are able to grasp essential facts through directive online instruction, while in-class exploratory activities encourage critical thinking and the synthesis of diverse perspectives. This approach not only enhances engagement but also fosters a more comprehensive and nuanced understanding of the subject matter.

Case Study 2: Integrative Therapy Approaches

Scenario:

A therapist is working with a client who experiences chronic anxiety. The therapist uses an integrative approach, combining Cognitive-Behavioral Therapy (CBT) techniques (Directive Mode) with humanistic, person-centered approaches (Exploratory Mode) to address the client's needs holistically. The goal is to help the client manage symptoms while also exploring underlying issues and fostering personal growth.

Step-by-Step Walkthrough:

1. **Initial Assessment and Directive Intervention**:

    ◦ During the initial sessions, the therapist conducts a thorough assessment using structured questions to identify the client's anxiety triggers and thought patterns. The therapist might ask, "Can you describe a recent situation where you felt anxious? What thoughts were going through your mind at that time?"

    ◦ Based on the assessment, the therapist introduces CBT techniques, such as thought challenging and relaxation exercises, to help the client manage anxiety symptoms. These interventions are delivered in a directive manner: "When you notice these anxious thoughts, use the STOP technique: Stop, Take a breath, Observe your thoughts, and Proceed with a more balanced thought."

2. **Transition to Exploratory Mode**:

    ◦ As the client becomes more comfortable with managing their symptoms, the therapist shifts to the Exploratory Mode to address deeper, underlying issues. The therapist might say, "Let's explore where these thoughts are coming from. When did you first start feeling this way? How do these feelings connect to other experiences in your life?"

    ◦ The therapist encourages the client to reflect on their past and present experiences, helping them to uncover and understand the roots of their anxiety.

3. **Dynamic Integration During Sessions**:

   - Throughout the sessions, the therapist dynamically shifts between directive and exploratory approaches. For example, if the client struggles to apply a CBT technique, the therapist provides additional directive guidance: "Let's practice this technique together, step by step."
   - When the client expresses a desire to explore a new topic or emotion, the therapist uses the Exploratory Mode to facilitate that exploration: "You mentioned feeling overwhelmed recently. Let's talk more about what might be contributing to that feeling. What do you think it's related to?"

4. **Balancing Structured Techniques with Personal Exploration**:

   - The therapist carefully balances structured interventions with open-ended exploration. For instance, after a session focused on CBT techniques, the therapist might dedicate the next session to a more open discussion about the client's personal goals and values: "How do you see yourself moving forward from this point? What would a life with less anxiety look like for you?"

5. **Ongoing Reflection and Adjustment**:

   - The therapist regularly reflects with the client on the progress made and adjusts the therapeutic approach as needed. The therapist might ask, "How are the CBT techniques working for you? Do you feel ready to explore other areas of your life that might be contributing to your anxiety?"
   - This ongoing reflection allows for dynamic integration to

be fine-tuned according to the client's evolving needs and readiness for different therapeutic approaches.

Embedded Example:

Therapist Question: "We've been working on managing your anxiety with specific techniques, and you've made great progress. I'm curious—when you think about these techniques, what deeper feelings or experiences come to mind? Let's explore that together."

Outcome:

The dynamic integration of directive CBT techniques and exploratory humanistic approaches in therapy leads to both symptom management and personal growth. The client gains practical tools for managing anxiety while also exploring and addressing deeper emotional and psychological issues. This holistic approach facilitates long-term healing and empowers the client to take an active role in their therapeutic journey.

Case Study 3: Adaptive AI Systems in Customer Service

Scenario:

A large retail company implements an AI-powered customer service system designed to handle a wide range of customer inquiries. The system uses dynamic integration to switch between directive responses for straightforward inquiries and exploratory interactions for more complex or ambiguous customer issues. The goal is to improve user satisfaction and efficiency by tailoring the interaction to the specific needs of each customer.

Step-by-Step Walkthrough:

1. **Handling Standard Inquiries (Directive Mode)**:

   - When a customer asks a straightforward question, such as "What is the status of my order?" the AI uses the Directive Mode to provide a clear and concise response: "Your order is on its way and is expected to arrive by [specific date]. You can track your order here: [tracking link]."
   - The AI's response is direct, addressing the customer's

inquiry efficiently without requiring further interaction.

2. **Identifying Complex Issues (Exploratory Mode)**:

   - If the customer's inquiry is more complex, such as "I'm having trouble with my recent purchase, but I'm not sure what's wrong," the AI recognizes the need for a more exploratory approach. The AI responds with an open-ended question: "Can you describe the issue you're experiencing with your purchase? Let's figure out how we can help."
   - The AI encourages the customer to provide more details, facilitating a deeper exploration of the issue.

3. **Dynamic Integration in Real-Time**:

   - As the customer provides more information, the AI dynamically shifts between directive and exploratory modes. For example, if the customer describes a specific problem (e.g., "The product isn't charging properly"), the AI switches to Directive Mode to offer a solution: "Please try the following steps to troubleshoot the issue..."
   - If the issue remains unresolved or if the customer's response indicates uncertainty, the AI reverts to the Exploratory Mode: "If those steps don't work, would you like to explore other options, such as a replacement or refund?"

4. **Personalizing the Interaction**:

   - The AI uses the customer's interaction history to personalize the conversation. For returning customers with previous inquiries, the AI might say: "I see you had a similar issue last month. How did that get resolved? Let's explore if this could be related."
   - This personalization enhances the customer experience,

making the interaction feel more tailored and responsive to individual needs.

5. **Closing the Interaction**:

   ◦ Once the issue is resolved, the AI concludes the interaction with a directive, clear message: "Thank you for your patience. If you have any more questions, feel free to reach out. Have a great day!"
   ◦ The AI then offers the customer a brief survey to rate their experience, gathering feedback to further refine its dynamic integration strategy.

Embedded Example:

AI Response: "I'm sorry to hear you're having trouble with your purchase. Can you tell me more about the issue? Let's explore what might be causing this so we can find the best solution for you."

Outcome:

Dynamic integration in the AI-powered customer service system improves customer satisfaction by providing tailored responses that match the complexity of the inquiry. Simple questions are answered quickly with directive responses, while more complex issues are explored in depth, leading to more effective and satisfying resolutions. This approach reduces the need for human intervention, increases efficiency, and enhances the overall customer experience.

Conclusion

These case studies illustrate how the dynamic integration of directive and exploratory modes, as outlined in the Dual Mode Elicitation Model (DEM), can be effectively applied across different fields. Through detailed scenarios and step-by-step walkthroughs, this section provides practical guidance on implementing dynamic integration in blended learning, integrative therapy, and adaptive AI systems. By leveraging the strengths of both modes, professionals can create more effective, responsive, and engaging interactions, leading to improved outcomes in education, therapy, and customer service.

Case Studies: DEM in AI Systems

5.4 Case Studies: DEM in AI Systems

This section presents detailed scenarios and step-by-step walkthroughs to demonstrate how the Dual Mode Elicitation Model (DEM) can be practically applied in AI systems across different industries. These case studies include applications in virtual healthcare, financial advisory services, and e-commerce customer service. Each case study illustrates how the dynamic integration of directive and exploratory modes enhances the effectiveness and user experience of AI systems.

Case Study 1: Virtual Healthcare Assistant

Scenario:

A healthcare provider has developed a virtual healthcare assistant designed to support patients with chronic conditions, such as diabetes or hypertension. The AI system employs the Directive Mode for routine tasks like medication management and symptom monitoring while using the Exploratory Mode during consultations to explore the patient's lifestyle, preferences, and concerns. The goal is to enhance patient engagement, adherence to treatment plans, and overall health outcomes.

Step-by-Step Walkthrough:

1. **Medication Management (Directive Mode):**

   - The AI system starts the day by reminding the patient to take their medication. It provides a clear, directive message: "Good morning! It's time to take your 8 AM dose of Metformin. Please confirm once you've taken it."
   - The patient confirms the action, and the AI records the compliance. If the patient forgets, the AI sends a gentle

reminder: "Don't forget, it's important to take your
medication on time. Please take it now and confirm."

2. **Symptom Monitoring (Directive Mode)**:

    ◦ Later in the day, the AI prompts the patient to record their
      blood glucose levels: "Please check your blood sugar now
      and enter the reading."
    ◦ If the reading is within the normal range, the AI responds
      with a supportive message: "Great! Your blood sugar is
      within the target range. Keep up the good work."
    ◦ If the reading is high or low, the AI provides clear
      instructions: "Your blood sugar is above the target range.
      Please recheck in an hour and follow your doctor's
      guidelines on what to do if your levels remain high."

3. **Lifestyle Consultation (Exploratory Mode)**:

    ◦ During a scheduled consultation, the AI switches to the
      Exploratory Mode to engage the patient in a more in-
      depth conversation about their lifestyle. The AI might ask:
      "How have you been feeling overall? Are there any
      challenges you're facing with your diet or exercise
      routine?"
    ◦ The patient mentions difficulties in sticking to their
      exercise plan. The AI explores further: "Can you tell me
      more about what's making it hard to stay active? Let's see
      if we can find a solution that fits better with your lifestyle."
    ◦ The AI encourages the patient to share more details,
      leading to a personalized discussion on potential
      adjustments, such as incorporating short, manageable
      workouts into their daily routine.

4. **Dynamic Integration for Personalized Care**:

    ◦ The AI dynamically integrates directive and exploratory

modes throughout the consultation. For instance, after discussing the challenges with exercise, the AI may return to Directive Mode to offer specific advice: "Let's set a goal of a 10-minute walk after dinner three times a week. How does that sound?"

- If the patient seems uncertain, the AI reverts to the Exploratory Mode: "What concerns do you have about starting this new routine? Let's talk through them and see how we can make this work for you."

5. **Follow-Up and Adherence**:

- The AI schedules follow-up reminders and check-ins based on the conversation: "I'll check in with you in a few days to see how the new exercise routine is going. Remember, consistency is key, and I'm here to support you every step of the way."
- This dynamic integration ensures that the AI is not only providing instructions but also adapting to the patient's needs and preferences, fostering better adherence to the treatment plan.

Embedded Example:

AI Query (Exploratory Mode): "You mentioned having trouble with your diet. Can you share more about what foods you find most challenging to avoid? Let's explore some healthier alternatives together."

Outcome:

The dynamic integration of directive and exploratory modes in the virtual healthcare assistant enhances patient engagement and adherence to treatment plans. By combining clear instructions with personalized consultations, the AI system supports patients in managing their chronic conditions more effectively, leading to improved health outcomes.

Case Study 2: AI-Powered Financial Advisor

Scenario:

A financial services firm has developed an AI-powered financial advisor that helps users manage their investments. The AI uses the Directive Mode to provide specific recommendations based on the user's financial goals and risk tolerance. When users seek more information or express uncertainty, the system switches to the Exploratory Mode to discuss alternative investment strategies and answer questions. The goal is to enhance informed decision-making and increase user confidence in managing their finances.

Step-by-Step Walkthrough:

1. **Initial Financial Assessment (Directive Mode)**:

   - When a user first interacts with the AI, the system begins with a directive assessment of their financial situation: "Let's start by reviewing your current portfolio. Based on your financial goals and risk tolerance, I recommend increasing your exposure to diversified index funds."
   - The AI provides clear, actionable advice: "You currently have 20% in cash reserves. I suggest moving 10% of this into a high-yield bond fund to optimize returns while maintaining liquidity."

2. **Exploring User Preferences (Exploratory Mode)**:

   - If the user is unsure about the recommendation, they might ask, "Why should I move cash into bonds? What are the risks involved?" The AI then switches to the Exploratory Mode: "That's a great question. Let's explore the benefits and risks together. What concerns you most about investing in bonds?"
   - The AI engages the user in a dialogue, asking open-ended questions to understand their concerns and preferences better: "Are you more interested in preserving capital or maximizing returns? Let's discuss how different

investment strategies align with your financial goals."

3. **Dynamic Integration for Tailored Advice**:

   - Based on the user's responses, the AI dynamically
     integrates the Directive Mode to offer specific advice:
     "Given your preference for capital preservation, I
     recommend starting with a conservative allocation. How
     about we move 5% into bonds and revisit this strategy in a
     few months?"
   - If the user remains hesitant, the AI continues in the
     Exploratory Mode: "Would you like to explore alternative
     investment options? Let's consider other low-risk assets
     that might suit your needs better."

4. **Scenario Analysis and Decision Support**:

   - The AI provides scenario analysis to help the user make
     informed decisions: "Let's compare how your portfolio
     might perform with the current allocation versus adding
     bonds. Here's a projected return analysis based on
     historical data."
   - The AI encourages the user to reflect on the analysis and
     offers further guidance based on the user's level of
     comfort: "Does this projection help clarify your decision?
     If you're still unsure, we can explore more conservative
     strategies or keep your portfolio as is for now."

5. **Continuous Engagement and Portfolio Monitoring**:

   - The AI sets up alerts and reminders to keep the user
     engaged and informed: "I'll monitor your portfolio and
     notify you of any significant market changes that might
     impact your investments. We can revisit your strategy
     whenever you're ready."
   - This dynamic integration ensures that the AI adapts to the

user's changing needs and preferences, providing ongoing support for their financial journey.

Embedded Example:

User Query (Exploratory Mode): "I'm not sure if bonds are the right move for me. What other options do I have if I want to avoid high risk?"

AI Response (Exploratory Mode): "Let's explore some other low-risk options, like Treasury bills or money market funds. How do you feel about those compared to bonds?"

Outcome:

The dynamic integration of directive and exploratory modes in the AI-powered financial advisor enhances user confidence and decision-making. By providing clear recommendations and engaging users in personalized discussions, the AI system helps users manage their investments more effectively, leading to better financial outcomes and increased satisfaction.

Case Study 3: Customer Service AI for E-Commerce

Scenario:

An e-commerce platform has implemented an AI-powered customer service system designed to handle a wide range of customer inquiries. The AI uses the Directive Mode to guide customers through common tasks, such as tracking orders or processing returns. If the customer has a more complex query, the AI transitions to the Exploratory Mode, engaging in a dialogue to understand the issue and offer personalized solutions. The goal is to improve customer satisfaction and reduce the need for human intervention.

Step-by-Step Walkthrough:

1. **Handling Routine Inquiries (Directive Mode)**:

   - A customer initiates a chat with the AI to track their order. The AI responds in Directive Mode: "Please enter your order number, and I'll provide the current status."

- The customer provides the order number, and the AI quickly responds: "Your order is on its way and is expected to arrive by [specific date]. Is there anything else I can assist you with?"

2. **Transitioning to Exploratory Mode for Complex Queries**:

   - The customer replies, "I received the package, but one of the items is damaged. I'm not sure how to handle this." The AI recognizes that this query requires a more nuanced response and shifts to the Exploratory Mode: "I'm sorry to hear about the damaged item. Can you describe the issue in more detail? Let's find the best solution for you."
   - The AI engages the customer in a conversation, asking follow-up questions to understand the situation fully: "Which item is damaged, and how severe is the damage? Do you have a preference for a replacement, a refund, or store credit?"

3. **Dynamic Integration for Personalized Solutions**:

   - Based on the customer's responses, the AI dynamically integrates the Directive Mode to offer a specific solution: "Given the damage you described, I recommend processing a replacement. I can initiate that for you right now. Would you like to proceed with a replacement?"
   - If the customer expresses uncertainty, the AI continues in the Exploratory Mode: "If you're not sure, we can explore other options. Would you prefer to receive a refund or store credit instead?"

4. **Resolving the Issue and Providing Support**:

   - After the customer decides on a replacement, the AI confirms the action and provides next steps: "I've processed the replacement. You'll receive a confirmation email shortly. The new item should arrive in 3–5 business days. Is there anything else I can help with?"

- The AI also provides guidance on what to do with the damaged item: "Please hold onto the damaged item until the new one arrives. We'll include instructions on how to return it if needed."

5. **Continuous Improvement Through Feedback**:

- After resolving the issue, the AI asks the customer for feedback: "Thank you for your patience. How satisfied are you with the help you received today? Your feedback helps us improve our service."
- The AI uses this feedback to adjust its responses in future interactions, ensuring continuous improvement in customer service quality.

Embedded Example:

Customer Query (Exploratory Mode): "I'm not sure if I want a replacement or a refund. What are the pros and cons of each option?"

AI Response (Exploratory Mode): "A replacement ensures you get the product you originally wanted, but it may take a few days to arrive. A refund, on the other hand, will return the money to your account within a few business days, and you can choose a different item if you prefer. Which option aligns better with your current needs?"

Outcome:

The dynamic integration of directive and exploratory modes in the customer service AI enhances customer satisfaction by providing tailored responses based on the complexity of the inquiry. Routine tasks are handled efficiently with directive responses, while more complex issues are explored in depth, leading to more personalized and effective solutions. This approach reduces the need for human intervention and improves the overall customer experience.

Conclusion

These case studies illustrate how the Dual Mode Elicitation Model (DEM) can be effectively applied in AI systems across different industries. Through detailed scenarios and step-by-step walkthroughs, this section provides practical guidance on implementing dynamic integration in virtual healthcare assistants, financial advisors, and e-commerce customer service platforms. By leveraging the strengths of both directive and exploratory modes, AI systems can enhance user engagement, satisfaction, and outcomes in a wide range of applications.

Case Studies and Practical Applications of DEM in Education

9.5 Case Studies and Practical Applications of DEM in Education

This section presents detailed scenarios and step-by-step walkthroughs to demonstrate how the Dual Mode Elicitation Model (DEM) can be effectively applied in educational settings. These case studies include applications in flipped classrooms, project-based learning in social studies, and differentiated instruction in mixed-ability classrooms. Each case study illustrates how the dynamic integration of directive and exploratory modes enhances teaching and learning outcomes.

Case Study 1: Flipped Classroom Model

Context:

A high school science teacher implements a flipped classroom model, where students are introduced to new material through instructional videos (Directive Mode) at home and then engage in exploratory, hands-on activities during class time. The goal is to maximize classroom time for interactive learning while ensuring that all students have a solid understanding of the foundational concepts before coming to class.

Step-by-Step Walkthrough:

1. **Pre-Class Preparation (Directive Mode)**:

   - **Instructional Videos**: The teacher creates and assigns instructional videos that cover the foundational concepts of the current unit, such as the principles of chemical reactions. The videos are clear, concise, and structured to ensure that students can easily grasp the material.

- **Follow-Up Quiz**: After watching the videos, students complete an online quiz that checks their understanding of the key concepts. The quiz provides immediate feedback, reinforcing the material and identifying areas where students may need additional review.

2. **Classroom Transition to Exploratory Mode**:

- **Lab Activities**: When students arrive in class, the teacher begins with a brief review based on the quiz results, addressing any common misconceptions. The teacher then introduces a hands-on lab activity where students can explore the concepts they learned at home. For example, students might conduct experiments to observe different types of chemical reactions.
- **Group Projects**: Students are grouped together and given a project related to the day's topic, such as designing and conducting their own experiment to demonstrate a specific reaction. The teacher circulates the room, using the Exploratory Mode to ask open-ended questions: "What do you predict will happen when you mix these chemicals? How could you design an experiment to test your hypothesis?"

3. **Dynamic Integration During Class**:

- **Real-Time Support**: As students work on their projects, the teacher shifts dynamically between directive and exploratory modes based on the needs of each group. For example, if a group struggles with the experimental design, the teacher provides more direct guidance: "Remember the steps we discussed for setting up a controlled experiment. Let's review those together."
- **Encouraging Exploration**: For students who are progressing well, the teacher remains in the Exploratory

Mode, encouraging them to test different variables and consider broader implications: "What other factors might influence the rate of reaction? How could you modify your experiment to explore this further?"

4. **Synthesis and Reflection**:

    ◦ **Class Discussion**: After the hands-on activities, the class reconvenes for a discussion. The teacher facilitates a dialogue where students share their findings and reflect on what they learned. The teacher prompts students to connect their practical experiences with the theoretical concepts from the videos: "How did your results compare with what you expected based on the video? What new questions do you have after doing the lab?"
    ◦ **Reflective Writing**: As homework, students are asked to write a brief reflection on the day's activities, integrating the concepts they learned at home with the insights gained during the lab. This reflective exercise helps solidify their understanding and encourages deeper thinking.

Embedded Example:

Teacher Question (Exploratory Mode): "You observed that the reaction rate increased when you added more of the catalyst. Why do you think that happened? What would happen if you doubled the amount of catalyst?"

Outcome:

The dynamic integration of directive and exploratory modes in the flipped classroom model leads to increased student engagement and a deeper understanding of scientific concepts. Students benefit from clear, structured instruction at home, which prepares them for interactive, hands-on learning in class. This approach not only reinforces foundational knowledge but also fosters creativity, critical thinking, and collaboration during in-class activities.

Case Study 2: Project-Based Learning in Social Studies

  Context:

A social studies teacher adopts a project-based learning approach to explore the impact of global trade on local communities. The project requires students to research, analyze, and present their findings on how trade policies affect different stakeholders. The goal is to develop students' critical thinking, research, and presentation skills while deepening their understanding of complex social and economic issues.

  Step-by-Step Walkthrough:

1. **Introduction to Project (Directive Mode)**:

   - **Lecture on Key Concepts**: The teacher begins by delivering a structured lecture on the basics of global trade, including key terms like tariffs, trade agreements, and supply chains. The lecture is designed to provide students with the essential knowledge they need to start their research.

   - **Guided Research**: The teacher provides students with a list of reputable sources and research questions to guide their initial exploration. For example, "How do trade tariffs affect local farmers? What role do trade agreements play in shaping the economy of developing countries?"

2. **Transition to Exploratory Mode**:

   - **Student-Led Research**: After the initial guidance, students are encouraged to dive deeper into their chosen topics. The teacher shifts to the Exploratory Mode, offering support as students pursue their research: "What new perspectives have you discovered in your research? How do these perspectives challenge or reinforce what we discussed in the lecture?"

   - **Collaboration and Discussion**: Students work in groups to analyze their findings and develop a cohesive narrative. The teacher circulates the room, asking probing questions to encourage critical thinking: "How do different stakeholders—such as businesses, consumers, and governments—benefit or suffer from these trade policies?"

3. **Dynamic Integration During Project Development**:

   - **Providing Structure When Needed**: As students work on their presentations, the teacher provides structured support to those who need it, such as helping to organize their findings or clarify their arguments. For example, "Let's structure your presentation so that you start with an overview of the issue, followed by case studies, and then conclude with your analysis."
   - **Encouraging Independent Thought**: For more advanced students, the teacher remains in the Exploratory Mode, prompting them to consider alternative perspectives and make connections between their research and broader social issues: "How does this trade policy reflect the balance of power between nations? What are the long-term implications for local communities?"

4. **Presentation and Reflection**:

   - **Student Presentations**: Each group presents their findings to the class. The teacher facilitates a Q&A session where other students can ask questions and challenge the presenters to defend their conclusions. This interactive component encourages a deeper exploration of the topic.
   - **Reflective Debrief**: After the presentations, the class engages in a reflective discussion. The teacher uses this time to integrate the directive and exploratory modes, helping students to connect their research with the broader concepts covered in the course: "How did this

project change your understanding of global trade? What were the most surprising insights you gained?"

Embedded Example:

Teacher Prompt (Exploratory Mode): "You've identified several ways that trade agreements can benefit large corporations. What about small businesses? How do you think they are impacted, and why might their experiences differ?"

Outcome:

The dynamic integration of directive and exploratory modes in project-based learning enables students to develop a deeper understanding of global trade and its impact on local communities. Students are guided through the initial stages of research but are encouraged to think critically and independently as they develop their projects. This approach fosters not only academic skills but also a nuanced understanding of complex social issues.

Case Study 3: Differentiated Instruction in a Mixed-Ability Classroom

Context:

A language arts teacher uses differentiated instruction to meet the needs of students with varying levels of ability and learning styles in a mixed-ability classroom. The goal is to provide all students with the appropriate level of challenge and support, ensuring that each student can progress at their own pace.

Step-by-Step Walkthrough:

1. **Initial Assessment and Grouping (Directive Mode)**:

   - **Pre-Assessment**: The teacher begins by administering a pre-assessment to gauge each student's reading and writing abilities. Based on the results, students are grouped into different levels: those needing additional support, those at grade level, and those ready for more advanced work.

- **Structured Mini-Lessons**: For students needing extra help, the teacher provides targeted mini-lessons that focus on specific skills, such as reading comprehension or essay structure. These lessons are delivered in the Directive Mode, ensuring that students receive clear and focused instruction.

2. **Transition to Exploratory Mode for Advanced Students**:

   - **Independent Projects**: Advanced students are given more freedom to explore topics of interest through independent reading and writing projects. The teacher shifts to the Exploratory Mode, offering guidance as these students choose their topics and research materials: "What themes are you most interested in exploring in your essay? How might you connect these themes to the texts we've studied in class?"

   - **Peer Collaboration**: The teacher encourages collaboration among advanced students, prompting them to discuss their ideas and provide feedback to each other: "How does your classmate's interpretation of the text differ from yours? What new perspectives can you gain from this discussion?"

3. **Dynamic Integration for Tailored Support**:

   - **Scaffolding Techniques**: For students who struggle with certain tasks, the teacher provides scaffolding, gradually reducing support as the students gain confidence. For example, "Let's work on the introduction of your essay together. We'll outline it now, and you can fill in the details later. Once you're comfortable, you can try the next section on your own."

   - **Encouraging Independent Exploration**: For students who are progressing well, the teacher uses the Exploratory

Mode to encourage deeper analysis and self-directed learning: "You've made some great points in your essay. What other texts or sources could you bring in to support your argument? How can you expand on your ideas?"

4. **Assessment and Reflection**:

    ◦   **Ongoing Assessment**: The teacher uses formative assessments, such as peer reviews and draft submissions, to monitor each student's progress and adjust instruction as needed. The teacher might provide directive feedback to guide students: "Your thesis is strong, but your argument would benefit from more textual evidence. Let's look at where you can incorporate quotes from the text."
    ◦   **Reflective Journals**: As a reflective exercise, students are asked to keep journals where they write about their learning experiences, challenges, and successes. The teacher reads these journals and uses the insights to further tailor instruction: "I noticed in your journal that you're finding the essay challenging. Let's meet to discuss how I can support you more effectively."

Embedded Example:

Teacher Feedback (Directive Mode): "Your analysis of the main character is insightful, but it needs more supporting evidence. Let's find some passages in the text that back up your points. We'll start with one example together, and then you can find another on your own."

Outcome:

The dynamic integration of directive and exploratory modes in differentiated instruction allows the teacher to meet the diverse needs of students in a mixed-ability classroom. Students who need more support receive clear, structured guidance, while more advanced students are encouraged to explore topics independently and engage in deeper analysis. This approach leads to improved outcomes for all students, as instruction is tailored to each individual's level of ability and learning style.

Conclusion

These case studies illustrate how the Dual Mode Elicitation Model (DEM) can be effectively applied in educational settings to enhance teaching and learning outcomes. Through detailed scenarios and step-by-step walkthroughs, this section provides practical guidance on implementing dynamic integration in flipped classrooms, project-based learning, and differentiated instruction. By leveraging the strengths of both directive and exploratory modes, educators can create more engaging, responsive, and effective learning environments that meet the needs of all students.

Interdisciplinary Research Database for DEM

1. **Cognitive Psychology**

Foundational Research:

1. **Kahneman, D. (2011). *Thinking, Fast and Slow*. New York: Farrar, Straus and Giroux.**

   - **Contribution**: This seminal work introduces the dual-process theory, which forms the conceptual basis for DEM's Directive and Exploratory Modes. Kahneman's distinction between System 1 (fast, intuitive thinking) and System 2 (slow, deliberate thinking) provides a framework for understanding how DEM can optimize communication by leveraging these cognitive processes.
   - **Application**: DEM integrates System 1 processing in the Exploratory Mode, encouraging creativity and adaptability, while System 2 processing is reflected in the Directive Mode, promoting structured, goal-oriented communication.

2. **Sweller, J. (1988). Cognitive load during problem solving: Effects on learning. *Cognitive Science*, 12(2), 257-285.**

   - **Contribution**: Sweller's Cognitive Load Theory explains how instructional design can affect learning efficiency, which is critical for understanding how DEM's Directive Mode can be used to manage cognitive load during communication.
   - **Application**: In DEM, Cognitive Load Theory informs the

structuring of information in the Directive Mode to optimize clarity and prevent cognitive overload, particularly in educational and AI settings.

1. **Gendron, M., & Barrett, L. F. (2018). Emotion perception as conceptual synchrony.** *Emotion Review,* **10(2), 101-110.**

   - **Contribution**: This research explores how emotions are perceived and constructed, offering insights into how emotional intelligence can be integrated into DEM, particularly in understanding how emotions influence communication.
   - **Application**: In DEM, this research underpins strategies for integrating emotional awareness into both the Directive and Exploratory Modes, ensuring communication is both effective and empathetic.

2. **Simmons, J. P., Nelson, L. D., & Simonsohn, U. (2018). False-positive psychology: Undisclosed flexibility in data collection and analysis allows presenting anything as significant.** *Psychological Science,* **29(5), 744-756.**

   - **Contribution**: This study highlights the importance of rigorous data practices, influencing how DEM can incorporate robust methodologies to ensure reliable outcomes, particularly in AI and data-driven applications.
   - **Application**: DEM can apply these principles to enhance the credibility of communication strategies, especially in research-based contexts where data integrity is paramount.

2. **Neuroscience**

Foundational Research:

1. **Kandel, E. R. (2006).** *In Search of Memory: The Emergence of a New Science of Mind.* **New York: W.W. Norton & Company.**

   - **Contribution**: Kandel's work on neural plasticity provides essential insights into how the brain adapts to new experiences, which is crucial for understanding the adaptability of communication strategies in DEM.
   - **Application**: Neural plasticity informs DEM's approach to fostering adaptable communication methods that can evolve based on new information and contexts.

2. **LeDoux, J. E. (1996).** *The Emotional Brain: The Mysterious Underpinnings of Emotional Life.* **New York: Simon & Schuster.**

   - **Contribution**: LeDoux's exploration of the neuroscience of emotion regulation is vital for integrating emotional dynamics into DEM, particularly in how emotions can be managed to optimize communication outcomes.
   - **Application**: DEM uses this research to guide the development of emotionally intelligent communication strategies that can be employed in both Directive and Exploratory Modes.

1. **Gallagher, S. (2005).** *How the Body Shapes the Mind.* **Oxford: Clarendon Press.**

   - **Contribution**: Gallagher's work on embodied cognition examines how physical experiences shape cognitive processes, providing a foundation for integrating physicality into communication strategies within DEM.
   - **Application**: Embodied cognition is leveraged in DEM to enhance the effectiveness of communication, particularly in contexts where physical presence and non-verbal cues play a critical role.

2. **Carhart-Harris, R. L., et al. (2014). The entropic brain: A theory of conscious states informed by neuroimaging research with psychedelic drugs.** *Frontiers in Human Neuroscience, 8, 20.*

   - **Contribution**: This study offers a novel perspective on consciousness and brain function, which can be used to inform the Exploratory Mode in DEM, particularly in fostering creativity and open-ended thinking.
   - **Application**: The entropic brain theory supports DEM's approach to promoting flexible, exploratory communication strategies that can adapt to complex and novel situations.

3. **Communication Theory**

Foundational Research:

1. **Korzybski, A. (1933).** *Science and Sanity: An Introduction to Non-Aristotelian Systems and General Semantics.* **New York: Institute of General Semantics.**

   - **Contribution**: Korzybski's General Semantics emphasizes the role of language in shaping reality, which is central to understanding how communication structures in DEM influence human interaction.
   - **Application**: DEM incorporates the principles of General Semantics to ensure that language use in both Directive and Exploratory Modes is precise, adaptable, and contextually appropriate.

2. **Shannon, C. E., & Weaver, W. (1949).** *The Mathematical Theory of Communication.* **Urbana: University of Illinois Press.**

   - **Contribution**: This foundational text introduces the

concept of communication as a mathematical and technical process, providing a basis for understanding how information is transmitted and received, which is integral to DEM.

- ◦ **Application**: DEM applies Shannon and Weaver's theories to optimize the transmission of information in the Directive Mode, ensuring that messages are clear, concise, and effectively communicated.

1. **Tomasello, M. (2019). *Becoming Human: A Theory of Ontogeny*. Cambridge, MA: Harvard University Press.**

   - ◦ **Contribution**: Tomasello's research on the development of communication in humans provides insights into the evolutionary basis of cooperative communication, which can inform DEM's strategies for fostering collaboration.
   - ◦ **Application**: DEM uses these insights to enhance the Exploratory Mode, particularly in contexts that require collaborative problem-solving and teamwork.

2. **Picard, R. W. (1997). *Affective Computing*. Cambridge, MA: MIT Press.**

   - ◦ **Contribution**: Picard's pioneering work on affective computing explores how machines can recognize and respond to human emotions, which is critical for the development of AI systems using DEM.
   - ◦ **Application**: DEM integrates affective computing principles to enhance AI-driven communication, ensuring that systems can respond empathetically and effectively to human users.

4. **AI Development**

Foundational Research:

1. **Mead, C. (1990).** *Neuromorphic Electronic Systems.* **Proceedings of the IEEE, 78(10), 1629-1636.**

   - **Contribution**: Mead's work on neuromorphic computing provides a foundation for AI systems that mimic the neural structures of the human brain, which is essential for developing AI that operates within the DEM framework.
   - **Application**: DEM utilizes neuromorphic computing to create AI systems that can dynamically integrate Directive and Exploratory Modes, adapting to user inputs in a human-like manner.

2. **Russell, S., & Norvig, P. (2010).** *Artificial Intelligence: A Modern Approach (3rd ed.).* **Upper Saddle River, NJ: Prentice Hall.**

   - **Contribution**: This comprehensive textbook on AI provides an in-depth overview of the algorithms and techniques that underpin modern AI systems, many of which are relevant to the implementation of DEM in AI contexts.
   - **Application**: DEM applies the principles outlined in this text to develop AI systems that can handle complex communication tasks, balancing structured guidance with adaptive, open-ended interactions.

1. **Gunning, D., et al. (2019).** *XAI–Explainable artificial intelligence.* **Science Robotics, 4(37), eaay7120.**

   - **Contribution**: This research on explainable AI (XAI) highlights the importance of transparency in AI decision-making, which is crucial for implementing DEM in AI systems that require user trust and understanding.
   - **Application**: DEM integrates XAI principles to ensure that AI systems can explain their actions in a way that users can understand, fostering trust and enhancing the overall

effectiveness of the system.

2. **Zeng, J., et al. (2020).** *The role of AI in responding to COVID-19.* **The Lancet Digital Health, 2(10), e482-e483.**

   - ◦ **Contribution**: This study examines the role of AI in managing public health crises, providing insights into how AI can be adapted to rapidly changing situations, which is relevant for the adaptive capabilities of DEM.
   - ◦ **Application**: DEM leverages this research to develop AI systems that can respond dynamically to emerging challenges, such as public health emergencies, by integrating both directive and exploratory approaches.

Ethical Guidelines and Best Practices

To ensure the responsible application of DEM, the following ethical guidelines and best practices have been developed, particularly focusing on privacy, autonomy, and the ethical implications of AI decision-making.

1. **Privacy**

Guideline:
Respect and protect the privacy of individuals by ensuring that all data collected and used within DEM applications, particularly in AI and healthcare, is handled with the utmost care.

   Best Practice Example:

- **Data Minimization**: Only collect data that is absolutely necessary for the specific DEM application. For example, in a healthcare setting, gather only the health information needed to provide personalized care, and ensure that this data is securely stored and only accessible to authorized personnel.

2. **Autonomy**

Guideline:
Uphold the autonomy of individuals by allowing them to make informed decisions about their participation in DEM processes, whether in education, AI interactions, or therapeutic settings.

   Best Practice Example:

- **Informed Consent**: Before implementing DEM in AI systems that interact with users, ensure that users are fully informed about how their data will be used and how the AI's decisions will affect them. Provide clear options for opting in or out of certain data uses or automated decision-making processes.

3. Ethical Implications of AI Decision-Making

Guideline:
Ensure that AI systems using DEM principles operate transparently and fairly, avoiding biases that could lead to unethical outcomes.
Best Practice Example:

- **Algorithmic Transparency**: Implement explainable AI (XAI) principles, where the AI system provides clear, understandable explanations for its decisions. For instance, if an AI financial advisor recommends a particular investment strategy, it should explain the reasoning behind the recommendation in a way that the user can understand and question.

Appendix: Advanced DEM Examples

This appendix provides a few advanced examples of how the Dual Mode Elicitation Model (DEM) can be applied in both human-human and human-AI interactions. These examples are designed to introduce more complex scenarios, demonstrating how DEM can be extended beyond basic applications to handle nuanced, dynamic interactions.

Advanced Human-Human Interaction Examples

Example 1: Complex Conflict Resolution in a Workplace Setting

Context:

A senior manager is mediating a conflict between two team leaders who have differing visions for a project. The goal is to use DEM to navigate the discussion, ensuring both parties feel heard (Exploratory Mode) while also guiding them toward a practical resolution (Directive Mode).

Scenario:

Manager (Directive Mode):

"Thank you both for coming. We need to find a way forward that aligns with our project goals. Let's start by hearing each of your perspectives. I'd like you both to focus on the specific outcomes you're aiming for."

Team Leader 1:

"I believe our priority should be to meet the deadline, even if it means compromising on some of the features. The client values timeliness over everything else."

Team Leader 2:

"I understand the deadline is important, but I think the quality of the features is what will set us apart. We can't afford to deliver a product that doesn't meet the highest standards."

Manager (Shifting to Exploratory Mode):

"It sounds like you both have valid concerns. Let's explore these priorities in more depth. What do you see as the potential risks and benefits of prioritizing the deadline over the features, and vice versa?"

Team Leader 1:

"The risk is delivering something that's incomplete, which could harm our reputation. But the benefit is maintaining our client's trust by delivering on time."

Team Leader 2:

"If we rush, we might deliver on time but at the cost of future business due to subpar quality. However, if we take a bit more time, we could ensure the client's satisfaction in the long term."

Manager (Dynamic Integration):

"Both points are crucial. Let's work together to find a middle ground. Could we explore a phased delivery, where we meet the initial deadline with a core set of features, and then follow up with additional features in a subsequent release? How would that address both of your concerns?"

Team Leader 1:

"That could work. We'd meet the deadline and keep the client happy."

Team Leader 2:

"And we'd still have the opportunity to ensure the final product meets our quality standards."

Manager (Reinforcing Directive Mode):

"Excellent. Let's outline the specifics of this phased approach, including what will be delivered by the deadline and how we'll communicate the plan to the client. We'll also set up checkpoints to ensure the quality of the subsequent release. Does this plan align with both of your expectations?"

Outcome:

By integrating Directive and Exploratory Modes, the manager facilitated a resolution that addressed both team leaders' concerns while aligning with the project's overall goals. The conflict was resolved constructively, and the team leaders felt their perspectives were valued.

Example 2: Navigating Sensitive Conversations in Personal Relationships

Context:

A couple is discussing a sensitive topic—finances. One partner feels they should start saving more aggressively for the future, while the other wants to enjoy their income by spending more on travel and experiences.

Scenario:

Partner 1 (Directive Mode):

"We need to talk about our savings. I'm worried that if we don't start saving more now, we'll face difficulties later. I think we should set aside at least 20% of our income each month."

Partner 2:

"I get that saving is important, but I don't want to miss out on enjoying our lives now. Traveling and having experiences are just as important to me."

Partner 1 (Shifting to Exploratory Mode):

"I hear you. Let's explore why traveling and having these experiences are so important to you. How do they make you feel, and what value do they add to your life?"

Partner 2:

"Traveling makes me feel alive and connected to the world. It's something that brings us closer together, and I don't want to give that up."

Partner 1 (Exploratory Mode):

"That's a beautiful perspective. I hadn't thought about it that way. What if we tried to find a balance? Let's explore some ways we could continue to save while still making room for the travel experiences that matter so much to us."

Partner 2:

"I like the sound of that. Maybe we could plan our trips more strategically, finding ways to save on travel without compromising on the experience."

Partner 1 (Dynamic Integration):

"That's a great idea. We could allocate a specific portion of our budget to travel each year and agree on a savings plan that still allows us to prepare for the future. How about we review our budget together and see how we can make this work?"

Outcome:

By using DEM to balance the Directive and Exploratory Modes, the couple was able to have a constructive conversation about finances that respected both partners' values. They found a compromise that allowed them to prioritize both savings and meaningful experiences.

Advanced Human-AI Interaction Examples

Example 1: AI-Assisted Career Counseling

Context:

An AI-powered career counselor is helping a user navigate a complex career decision. The user is considering a major career shift and needs guidance on evaluating the risks and opportunities.

Scenario:

User:

"I'm thinking about leaving my current job to start my own business, but I'm not sure if it's the right move. Can you help me weigh the pros and cons?"

AI (Directive Mode):

"Let's start by outlining the key factors in your decision. We'll assess your financial stability, the market potential of your business idea, and your readiness to take on the challenges of entrepreneurship. First, can you provide an overview of your current financial situation?"

User:

"I have some savings, but not a lot of startup capital. I'm also unsure about the market demand for my business idea."

AI (Shifting to Exploratory Mode):

"Thank you for sharing that. Let's explore your motivations for starting this business. What excites you about this idea, and what do you hope to achieve by becoming an entrepreneur?"

User:

"I'm passionate about creating something of my own and having the freedom to work on my terms. I also believe there's a niche market that isn't being served well by current businesses."

AI (Exploratory Mode):

"Your passion and insight into a niche market are strong motivators. Let's delve deeper into the market potential. Would you like to explore some data on current trends in your target industry, or perhaps conduct a SWOT analysis (Strengths, Weaknesses, Opportunities, Threats) of your business idea?"

User:

"A SWOT analysis sounds helpful. I'd like to understand the risks better."

AI (Dynamic Integration):

"Let's start with the SWOT analysis. I'll guide you through each step. We'll identify your strengths, such as your industry knowledge, and weaknesses, like limited startup capital. Then, we'll look at opportunities in the market and potential threats, such as competition or economic downturns. Afterward, we can reassess your financial plan to see if there are ways to mitigate these risks while pursuing your entrepreneurial goals."

User:

"That sounds like a plan. I'm ready to get started."

Outcome:

The AI effectively used DEM to guide the user through a structured decision-making process while also encouraging exploration of personal motivations and market opportunities. The user gained a clearer understanding of the risks and rewards, leading to a more informed decision.

Example 2: AI-Enhanced Medical Diagnosis

Context:

A user is consulting with an AI-powered health assistant about a recurring health issue. The AI needs to provide both immediate, clear advice (Directive Mode) and engage the user in a detailed exploration of their symptoms and lifestyle (Exploratory Mode) to offer a comprehensive diagnosis.

Scenario:

User:

"I've been having frequent headaches lately. They're not severe, but they're persistent. What should I do?"

AI (Directive Mode):

"Based on the information you've provided, it's important to first rule out any immediate causes. Let's start by tracking the frequency and intensity of your headaches over the next week. I recommend that you avoid potential triggers such as caffeine and monitor your hydration levels. I'll help you log thcsc details."

User:

"Okay, I'll start tracking. But what could be causing these headaches?"

AI (Shifting to Exploratory Mode):

"Let's explore that together. There could be several contributing factors, including stress, diet, or even your environment. Have there been any recent changes in your lifestyle, such as increased stress at work or changes in your diet or sleep patterns?"

User:

"I've been working longer hours and skipping meals sometimes. I also haven't been sleeping well."

AI (Exploratory Mode):

"Those factors could certainly be contributing to your headaches. Let's examine each one in more detail. Would you like to start by exploring how your work schedule might be affecting your stress levels, or would you prefer to look at your sleep patterns first?"

User:

"Let's start with my sleep. I've been having trouble falling asleep and often wake up feeling tired."

AI (Dynamic Integration):

"Poor sleep can be a significant trigger for headaches. I can help you develop a sleep hygiene routine to improve your sleep quality. Let's set up a plan that includes a consistent bedtime, reducing screen time before bed, and perhaps incorporating relaxation techniques. We'll monitor your sleep and see if your headaches improve over the next few weeks. Does that sound like a good place to start?"

User:
"Yes, I'd like to try that. I'll follow the plan."

Outcome:
The AI used DEM to guide the user through both immediate actions and a deeper exploration of potential causes. This approach ensured that the user received practical advice while also considering underlying factors, leading to a more holistic approach to managing their health.

Conclusion

These advanced examples demonstrate how DEM can be applied in more complex human-human and human-AI interactions. By integrating Directive and Exploratory Modes dynamically, the communication becomes not only more effective but also more nuanced, addressing both immediate needs and underlying concerns. These examples provide a foundation for further exploration of advanced DEM applications, setting the stage for deeper engagement and more sophisticated use of the model.